AF556323

THE ATLANTIC CRITICAL STUDIES

WILLIAM SHAKESPEARE'S

The Tempest

THE ATLANTIC CRITICAL STUDIES

WILLIAM SHAKESPEARE'S
The Tempest

RATRI RAY

Published by

ATLANTIC

PUBLISHERS & DISTRIBUTORS (P) LTD

B-2, Vishal Enclave, Opp. Rajouri Garden,
New Delhi-110027
Phones : 25413460, 25429987, 25466842

Sales Office
7/22, Ansari Road, Darya Ganj,
New Delhi-110002
Phones : 23273880, 23275880, 23280451
Fax : 91-11-23285873
web : www.atlanticbooks.com
e-mail : info@atlanticbooks.com

Printed in India
at Nice Printing Press, Delhi

General Preface

The Atlantic Critical Studies, modelled on the study-aids available in England and America, among other places, are primarily meant for the students of English Literature of Indian universities.

However, in consideration of the local conditions and the various constraints under which our students have to study—non-availability of relevant critical books, dearth of foreign and Indian journals, inaccessibility to good, well-equipped libraries, just to mention a few of them—the models have been considerably improved upon, both qualitatively and quantitatively.

Thus, while these studies are meant to be comprehensive and self-sufficient, the distinguished scholars who have prepared these study materials, have taken special care to combine lucidity and profundity in their treatment of the texts.

The Select Bibliography at the end is meant not only to acknowledge the sources used but also to help a student in the pursuit of further studies if s/he wants to.

Atlantic Publishers & Distributors (P) Ltd., New Delhi believe in quality and excellence. These studies will only reconfirm it.

Mohit K. Ray
Chief Editor [English Literature]
Atlantic Publishers & Distributors,
New Delhi

Contents

1

Introduction

There is a widely prevalent notion that the greatness of a genius is recognised only posthumously, and further he generally dies in poverty. This idea though true in many cases is not true about Shakespeare. He, indeed, was recognised for what he was—a powerful genius who produced works of high excellence whatever the medium, sonnets, lyrics or plays. Not only did he get recognition from the poets and dramatists of his own time, but from the play-going public as well. His plays were highly successful on the stage, so much so that he bought a share in the company and also bought land and house in his native village. He died one of the richest men of his village. This shows how much his own age recognised his genius.

It is not that he lived for a long time, but within the few years that cover his productivity he poured out a stream of poems, plays and sonnets such as have been hardly equalled. There were many rules and conventions in drama that he had to follow and sometimes, as in *The Tempest,* he followed them. At other times he soared above all rules and customs and still produced works that have triumphantly withstood the onslaught of time. Different elements, like the plot, the characters, the theme, etc. blend in each of his plays to harmonise into a many-coloured, rainbow-like brilliance. The more one reads his plays, the more beauties one discovers. Words like "sublimity", "universality", "esemplastic imagination", etc. describe only different aspects of his genius. He remains inexhaustible.

He registers a surprising range and variety in the field of drama itself. He excelled in whatever genre he took up. He has written plays of all kinds, tragedies, comedies and histories, which cannot be said of any other writer of his time. His greatest rival Marlowe wrote only tragedies, and Ben Jonson was successful only in his satirical comedies. Within these three main genres of contemporary plays, again, there is more variety in Shakespeare than in anyone else. All the four main kinds of tragedy can be found in his works. The conqueror tragedy is presented by *Macbeth,* the Revenge tragedy by *Hamlet*, the Villain tragedy by *Othello* and the Domestic by *Romeo and Juliet.* Likewise we have Romantic comedies (*Twelfth Night*), Pastoral comedies (*As You Like It*), Problem comedies (*Measure for Measure*) and Romances like the play that is going to be studied. It must always be remembered that these labels do not exhaust the possibilities of his highly complex plays. He took up a popular genre, perfected his art at it, and soared high above all its limitations.

In all, he wrote sixteen comedies, not counting *Merry Wives of Windsor* which is categorised as a farce. They are divided into four groups as follows:

(1) The Early Comedies—*The Two Gentlemen of Verona, The Comedy of Errors, Love's Labour's Lost, A Midsummer Night's Dream.*

(2) The Golden Comedies—*The Merchant of Venice, Much Ado About Nothing. As You Like It, Twelfth Night.*

(3) The Problem Comedies—*Measure for Measure, Troilus and Cressida, All's Well that Ends Well, Timon of Athens.*

(4) The Last Romances—*Pericles, Cymbeline, The Winter's Tale, The Tempest.*

It is significant that Shakespeare's dramatic career began and ended with comedies. Comedy does not merely mean the love and the marriage of the hero and the heroine. It essentially signifies the triumph of good over evil. The French critic Henri Fluchère points this out:

> What has always appealed to him with constant tenacity is the haunting sense of order and equilibrium which can be

attained only by crushing the forces of evil by the triumph of the good.[1]

REFERENCE

1. Fluchère, H. *Shakespeare*. London: Longmans Green & Co., 1953, p. 264.

2

The Background

(a) The Socio-Political Background

It has been asserted by the great social historian G.M. Trevelyan that Shakespeare's works have immediate and integral relationship with his time:

> His works could never have been produced in any other period than those late Elizabethan and early Jacobean times in which it was his luck to live. He could not have written as he did if the men and women among whom his days were passed had been other than they were.[1]

It is necessary to know the socio-political background of any writer before one can hope to understand his work. A brief chronological table from the time of Queen Elizabeth's succession to the throne of England to the death of our poet is given below. It contains the main political, social and religious events of the time.

A CHRONOLOGICAL TABLE

1558	–	Queen Mary I dies. Elizabeth I succeeds.
	–	Mary Queen of the Scots marries the French Dauphin.
'59	–	Mary Queen of the Scots declares herself Queen of England. War between Spain and France ends.
	–	Church of England re-established more firmly.
'60	–	The Scottish Parliament establishes the Reformed Church and breaks with Rome.

1561	–	Mary Queen of Scots returns from France. She clashes with the Calvinists.
'62	–	The Huguenots begin emigrating from France to England.
'63	–	Bubonic plague in Europe.
'64	–	*Shakespeare born.* Anglo-French war ends. England at war with Spain. Galileo born.
	–	The Thirty-Nine Articles adopted by the Church of England. Queen Elizabeth tries to enforce uniformity of religion.
'67	–	Mary Queen of Scots abdicates. Rugby Chapel founded.
'68	–	Mary Queen of Scots flees to England and is held captive by Queen Elizabeth.
'69	–	Rebellion of the Roman Catholic earls crushed.
'70	–	Pope Pius V excommunicates Queen Elizabeth.
'74	–	Burbage gets license for the first theatre in London.
'76	–	Tycho Brahe begins his astronomical observations.
	–	Burbage opens the first theatre in London.
'77	–	Treaty with the Dutch signed. Sir Francis Drake begins his circumnavigation of the world.
'80	–	Sir Francis Drake completes circumnavigation.
'81	–	Conversion to Catholicism declared to be treason.
	–	Galileo discovers Law of the Pendulum.
'83	–	Plot against the Queen. Humphrey Gilbert takes possession of Newfoundland for England.
'84	–	Sir Walter Raleigh discovers, names and colonizes Virginia.
'86	–	England wins the battle of Zutphen in which Sir Philip Sidney dies.
	–	Plot against the Queen. Mary Queen of Scots implicated and convicted of treason.

1587	–	Rose Theatre built by Henslowe.
'88	–	Defeat of the Spanish Armada by Drake.
'89	–	Galileo publishes the results of his experiments with falling bodies.
'92	–	John Davis discovers the Falkland islands.
'93	–	Absence from the church on Sundays made punishable by law.
'95	–	Southwell the mystical poet executed for celebrating Mass.
'96	–	England, France and Netherlands form alliance against Spain.
'97	–	Irish rebellion. Statutory provision for Poor Relief. Beggary made illegal.
'98	–	The Bodleian Library begun. Globe Theatre opened.
1603	–	Queen Elizabeth dies. Accession of King James I.
'04	–	Peace with Spain.
	–	Acts against priests and recusants. Anglican canons made.
'05	–	Repression of Puritans and Catholics. Gunpowder plot.
'08	–	Failure of plan for union with Scotland.
'10	–	Judicial decision against royal proclamations.
'11	–	Parliament dissolved.
'12	–	Alliance with German Protestant princes.
	–	Witches hanged at Lancashire.
'16	–	*Shakespeare dies.*

A careful study of this table presents a fairly clear picture of the contemporary socio-political situation. At the time when Shakespeare was born, the throne of England was in a highly unstable condition. There were plots against the Queen at home and constant warfare with the neighbouring nations abroad. It took the Queen quite a few years to consolidate her position and bring political stability to England. Her policies, both at home and abroad, were tolerant ones and she gradually brought peace and stability, which had made a wise contemporary call her "a shrewd, learned and moderate young woman". Even the controversies over religion came to an end under her wise governance. The establishing of a definite religion in England was one of her greatest achievements. As G.M. Trevelyan has pointed out:

> In the year in which the Queen succeeded her sister Mary, Puritanism was mainly a foreign doctrine imported from Geneva and Rhineland; when she died it was rootedly and characteristically English.[2]

The time of Queen Elizabeth is known as a time of peace and prosperity and expansion in every field. Thus, as far as the social structures are concerned, the class barriers did exist, but this was a feature that was generally accepted, and not resented by anyone. The feudal lords, except in rare cases, did not suppress the lower classes. G.M. Trevelyan has explained this attitude:

> English society was based not on equality but freedom—freedom of opportunity and freedom of personal intercourse. Such was the England known and approved by Shakespeare.[3]

In this society each individual earned a fair wage for honest labour and this, in its turn, bred self-reliance and self-respect. There were no bondmen, nor were there slaves.

Industrial prosperity was also one of the important features of this time. The factory system had just been started and the capitalist employer was anxious to keep his factory working at full capacity. Mining expanded to such an extent that metals which were formerly at a premium, like lead, copper, iron and tin, became easily available to all.

Sir Francis Drake brought national pride to great heights by his two famous achievements—the defeat of the Spanish Armada in 1688 and the circumnavigation of the globe which took nearly three years. A sense of joy and exuberance pervaded entire England and is reflected in the literature of the time. G.M. Trevelyan has given a succinct summing-up:

By the end of Elizabeth's reign not only was England commercially and financially thus reviving and expanding on a modern basis but her ancient rivals were in rapid decline.[4]

Another social movement which is of special importance as far as *The Tempest* is concerned is the colonising movement. King James I, in the very first year of his reign, made peace with Spain. This ensured the end of wartime hostilities and groups of settlers started crossing the seas in order to colonise the newly-acquired foreign lands like New England, Virginia, etc. One such expedition met with great misfortune in the shape of a terrible storm at sea and one of the ships was totally destroyed. An account of this storm was later written by one of the survivors and supplied material for the first scene of the play (*vide* the section on the sources of the play, Ch. 9, *infra*). Interest in new lands with the strange creatures in them was a common phenomenon.

(b) The Literary Background

The Elizabethan Age is known as the Golden Age of England. This is fully justified from many points of view. As has been seen above the age was prosperous from the socio-political point of view and it was equally so from the literary point of view as well. A chronological table is given below, covering the main literary events of the time. The table begins with the first performance of *Ralph Roister Doister,* ten years before Shakespeare was born. His own plays are not given here and will be given later.

A CHRONOLOGICAL TABLE

1554	–	Sir Philip Sidney and Lyly born.
	–	*Ralph Roister Doister* performed.
'57	–	Tottel's *Miscellany*.
'58	–	Kyd, Greene, Peele, Lodge born.
'61	–	Bacon born. *Gorboduc* performed.
'63	–	Drayton and Donne born.
'64	–	*Shakespeare born.* Marlowe born.

1565	–	Norton and Sackville's *Gorboduc*
'66	–	*Supposes* by Gascoigne.
	–	Udall, *Ralph Roister Doister.*
'67	–	Campion and Nashe born.
'75	–	Heywood and Tourneur born.
	–	*Appius and Virginia, Gammer Gurton's Needle.*
'76	–	*Paradyse of Daynty Devises.*
'77	–	Holinshed's *Chronicles.*
'79	–	*Shepheardes Calendar* by Spenser.
'85	–	Kyd's *Spanish Tragedy.*
'86	–	Sir Philip Sidney dies. Lyly's *Endimion.*
'87	–	Marlowe's *Tamburlaine,* Lyly's *Gallathea.*
'89	–	Marlowe's *Jew of Malta.*
'90	–	*Faerie Queene* Bks. I–III published.
'91	–	*Astrophel and Stella, Edward II.*
'92	–	Revised *Arcadia,* Daniel's *To Delia. Hero and Leander, Arden of Feversham.*
'95	–	*Amoretti, Epithalamion, Apology for Poetry.*
'98	–	Marlowe. *Hero and Leander.*
'99	–	Spenser dies.
1600	–	*England's Helicon, Cynthia's Revels.*
'01	–	Dekker and Marston's *Satiromastix,* Jonson's *Poetaster.*
'03	–	Dowland's *Third Book of Songs, Sejanus Woman Killed with Kindness, Dutch Courtezan.*
'04	–	Chapman's *Bussy D'Ambois,* Marston's *Malcontent.*
'05	–	Drayton's *Collected Poems,* Middleton's *A Trick to Catch the Old One.*
'06	–	Lyly dies. *Yorkshire Tragedy, Volpone,* Tourneur's *Revenger's Tragedy.*
'07	–	Beaumont & Fletcher's *Knight of the Burning Pestle.*

1608	–	Fuller and Milton born.
'09	–	Beaumont & Fletcher's *Philaster,* Fulke Greville's *Mustapha.*
'10	–	Ben Jonson's *The Alchemist* (perfomed; printed in 1612).
'11	–	Spenser's *Collected Works, The Authorised Version of the Bible, A King and No King.*
'12	–	Crashaw born. Chapman's *Iliad–I–XXIV*, Donne's *The Second Anniversarie.* Webster's *The White Devil.*
'13	–	Samuel Purchas. *Purchas: His Pilgrimage.*
'14	–	Overbury's *Characters,* Lodge's *Works of Seneca,* Sir Walter Raleigh's *History of the World.* Jonson's *Bartholomew Fair.* Webster's *The Duchess of Malfi.*
'16	–	Chapman's *The Whole Works of Homer*, Jonson's *Mercury Vindicated Epicene.*

The years covering the time from Shakespeare's birth in 1564 to his death in 1616 are the best years of the Elizabethan Age, though some are of the opinion that the date can be shifted back to Sidney's birth in 1554. This was definitely the best time from a literary point of view. In the Chronological Table given above the stress has fallen on poetry and drama, but many important prose works had also been published. Many of the numerous poetical and dramatic works also have not been mentioned, only a few, the most prominent, have been put there.

It has to be noted that during Sidney's lifetime the most well-known works had not yet been produced and so Sidney had a poor opinion about contemporary drama. During Shakespeare's childhood many plays were being written and staged—all of an inferior kind. *Gorboduc*, the only play for which Sidney has some good words to say in his *Apologie for Poetrie* was more Italian than English. In 1587 a play was performed for the Queen's entertainment, specially written for the occasion by a group of eight authors. This play, *The*

Misfortunes of King Arthur, has only historical value today. Such works have historical importance, with little dramatic value and cannot come up to what Shakespeare, Marlowe and the others were to write in literary excellence.

Not only in drama, but in sonnets, songs and narrative poems also Shakespeare had hardly any model, though in this respect, the situation is marginally better than in drama. Spenser's *Shepheardes Calendar* and the first few books of his *Faerie Queene* had already been published before Shakespeare wrote *Venus and Adonis,* his first narrative poem. The sonnets of Wyatt and Surrey had been published by Tottel in his famous *Miscellany*, and it was in the last decade of this century that the famous sequences of love-sonnets started to be written. Three of them, Sidney's *Astrophel and Stella*, Daniel's *To Delia* and Spenser's *Amoretti* have been mentioned in the table given above. From 1680 onwards the countless love-songs started being written. The poets, mostly anonymous, are today known as "the Elizabethan nest of singing-birds". Some of these collections have been included in the table above, like *The Paradyse of Daynty Devises, England's Helicon,* etc. There are many songs in Shakespeare where their influence can be traced.

The Elizabethan Age, as it advanced, poured forth a dazzling stream of many kinds of poems: narrative, lyrical, discursive, philosophical, religious, etc. Prose was also flourishing in the hands of writers like Bacon, Sir Thomas Browne, Burton, Hooker and others.

Our immediate concern is drama. Kyd's famous play *The Spanish Tragedy* was a revenge tragedy in the Senecan mode. It became instantly popular and soon came to be taken as a model for revenge tragedies. Another such popular tragedy was *Tamburlaine* with which Marlowe started his dramatic career. This was so successful that Marlowe had to produce a sequel to it and both, in their artistic excellence, bear the imprint of his genius. Burbage and later Henslowe, established theatre halls where plays were regularly performed. All the great dramatists honed their skill at these places. Experiments were made and developments in the many branches of the five-act form took place. Tragedies of four different kinds, comedies catering to three distinct classes of audience, chronicle plays and farces were being produced in great numbers. Shakespeare, Ben Jonson, Webster, Tourneur, Chapman, Beaumont and Fletcher and many others contributed some of their best works.

The tragedies of the time, designated as the 'blood-and-thunder tragedies', have been categorised into four sections: Conqueror tragedy, of the kind Marlowe wrote, Revenge tragedy started by the Spanish Tragedy, Villain tragedy, like Middleton and Rowley's *The Changeling* and Domestic tragedy, like *Arden of Feversham.* Many of these tragedies can come under more than one category. *Othello,* for example, can be called a villain tragedy as well as a domestic tragedy. This division is given by T. Spencer.

Comedy flourished in the hands of Ben Jonson, Shakespeare and many others. M.C. Bradbrook has divided the Elizabethan society into three sections, allotting a specific comedy to each. These social divisions are those of the Court, the Country and the City. The comedies of Shakespeare come mostly under the first category. Apart from these divisions there are other varieties within them as well. The romantic comedies of Shakespeare, known as the Golden comedies, as well as the Romances, to which category *The Tempest* belongs, are distinctly different from his Dark Comedies, though both were written for courtly audiences. Ben Jonson, Webster, Chapman, Marston wrote satirical comedies, whereas tragi-comedies were produced by Beaumont and Fletcher in collaboration. There was, thus, great variety in tragedy as well as comedy.

Another important variety of entertainment was the Masque. These masques were extremely popular works and were particularly used for celebrating happy occasions like betrothals, marriages, etc. These made use of mythical and supernatural characters like gods and goddesses, and therefore involved the use of gorgeous costumes. Naturally such productions became extremely expensive and were produced mainly by the aristocracy and at Court. Very often the aristocrats themselves took part in the masques, particularly in

Queen Elizabeth's court. The masques made use of song and dance and thus provided the element of spectacle as demanded by the classical rules. Ben Jonson together with the designer Inigo Jones, wrote many masques. These were produced independent of plays. Shakespeare incorporated masques within his plays, as he has done in *The Tempest*. This particular masque is dramatically important as it celebrates the betrothal of the hero and the heroine, and it also celebrates a royal wedding, thus serving a double purpose. The masque thus has a special importance.

Apart from these there were also numerous farces, providing laughter. These usually dealt with characters taken from the lower section of society. Shakespeare's *Merry Wives of Windsor*, written at the special wish of Queen Elizabeth, is commonly regarded as a farce and is the only play of this kind that he wrote.

REFERENCES

1. Trevelyan, G.M. *Illustrated English Social History*, Vol. 2, Harmondsworth: Penguin Books Ltd., p. 125.
2. *Ibid.*, p. 86
3. *Ibid.*, p. 62.
4. *Ibid.*, p. 123.

3

Life and Works

(a) A Short Biography

Not much is known about the writers of the Elizabethan Age. Very little, for example, is known about Ben Jonson and Webster. In comparison there is a wealth of such detail about Shakespeare that one can be certain of many dates and events in his life. This is because, as Irving Ribner has pointed out:

> As a dramatist Shakespeare acquired considerable reputation during his own lifetime. It continued to grow in the centuries following his death in 1616, accumulating as it did so an accretion of legends and anecdotes.[1]

The biographies of Shakespeare have been based on these legends, supported by the entries made in the village register and later from various other documents. A chronological table of the important events is given below:

A CHRONOLOGICAL TABLE OF THE CHIEF EVENTS OF SHAKESPEARE'S LIFE

1564	–	April 23, the supposed date of birth of Shakespeare.
	–	April 26, Shakespeare baptized.
'71	–	Possible time of enrolment in the Grammar School.
'78	–	His father suffers serious financial loss.
'82	–	Shakespeare is married to Anne Hathaway.
'83	–	Birth of Susannah, his first daughter.

1585 – Baptism of the twins, Hamnet and Judith.
'86 – Shakespeare's supposed departure for London.
'93 – *Venus and Adonis* published by a fellow villager.
'94 – *Rape of Lucrece, Titus Andronicus*
'96 – Tragic death of his only son Hamnet, at 12 years.
'97 – Shakespeare buys New Place.
'99 – He buys shares in the Globe Theatre.
1602 – The birth of his first grandchild. He buys one hundred and seven acres of land.
'04 – His company comes under royal patronage and is given the name of the King's Men.
'11 – He retires from the company and comes back to settle in his native village.
'13 – *The Tempest* staged.
'16 – Jan. 25 – His Last Will and Testament drawn up.
– Apr. 23 – Shakespeare dies on his 52nd birth anniversary.
– Apr. 25 – Buried in the Chancel of Stratford Church.

Though the exact date of his birth is not known, the date of his christening had been recorded in the Register of Baptism in the parish church of Stratford-upon-Avon. This Register records, in official Latin as given below:

1564, Apr. 26, Gulielmus Filius Johannes Shakspere.[2]

The spelling of the surname is different from today's, but it should be kept in mind that English was still a young language and spelling and grammar was still in a fluid condition. The same writer would spell the same word in two or three different ways in the same page.

It was the custom in those days to christen a baby three days after its birth, and therefore, it is generally assumed that Shakespeare was born on the twenty-third of April at Stratford-upon-Avon, in the county of Warwickshire. According to the

Christian religious calendar, this day was known as St. George's Day.

The next few years of Shakespeare's life are not documented. It is assumed that he led a happy and secure childhood in the bosom of a loving and prosperous family. His position in the family was an important one, for he was the eldest son, though the third child. His father, John Shakespeare, was a prosperous tradesman with a respected place in society. He eventually became the mayor of Stratford and later in 1565 the alderman. He, by this time, had reached such a high position that he could claim the status of a gentleman (*i.e.* the landed gentry as differentiated from a trader). Mary Arden, Shakespeare's mother, belonged to a family of the small landed gentry and was socially higher than his father.

The countryside around the village was unspoilt in those days and Shakespeare was able to have intimate contact with nature. Wonderful verbal picture of the English countryside can be found in his work, whose foundations were laid at this time. He carried the memory of the trees, flowers and animals to reproduce them repeatedly.

His father, often, had to take active part in judicial matters as he was not only a Justice of Peace but the High Bailiff of Stratford as well. Shakespeare, it is thought, must have accompanied him to the law courts and thus gained legal knowledge, which is evident in his writings.

Queen Elizabeth, in order to make education available to all, had established Grammar Schools all over England in the second half of this century. Stratford also had a well-established Grammar School where the classics were taught. No one can say for sure at what age Shakespeare was admitted to the local school—according to some he was seven years old at the time, and nine according to others. Roughly at about this time he was enrolled and acquired his store of classical knowledge. It is a well-known fact that Ben Jonson had no good opinion of his knowledge for he said that he had but "small Latin and less Greek" but the knowledge he acquired at the school he attended is not insignificant. He stayed at the school for nearly seven years. Here, too, biographers cannot say exactly when he left the school. He had a retentive memory and made repeated use of all that he learnt in his works.

Quite a respectable amount is known about the schools of the Elizabethan Age. They started at six in the morning in summer and at seven in winter, and went on till five in the evening. There were frequent breaks during the day, coming to a total of two and a half hours. The boys were taught mainly Latin grammar and literature. Shakespeare must have studied the following works which were in vogue at that time:

Poetry : Mantuan's *The Bucolica* in imitation of Virgil. Virgil's *Eclogues* and *The Aeneid.* Horace's *Poems* and Ovid's *Metamorphoses.*

Prose : Caesar, Livy and Cicero.

Drama : Seneca's *Ten Tragedies.*
The comedies of Plautus and Terence.

This curriculum seems to be more than enough for a schoolboy. Drawing attention to the amount of classical literature that was instilled into the students, I. Ribner has remarked:

> In the light of the training a normal schoolboy would have undergone at the Stratford Grammar School, it is difficult to understand why the extent of Shakespeare's learning has been so much a subject for debate.[3]

John Dover Wilson, however, disagrees with all these suppositions and holds the opinion that Shakespeare did not attend any of these schools because they were all administered by Protestants. John Shakespeare was, on the other hand, a devout Catholic. Dover Wilson holds that he would have put his son in the service of a Catholic nobleman where he would have gained, in addition to his education, a first-hand knowledge of the life-style of the nobility.

These were the formative years of his life and he gathered knowledge from various other sources as well. The great noblemen of the time, the Earls of Leicester and of Warwickshire, patronised theatrical companies which travelled all over the country. Shakespeare must have seen many plays enacted in his own village.

In his eighteenth year he came across Anne Hathaway who was twenty-six at the time. They got married on Nov. 28, 1582. Next year their first daughter Susannah was born and two years later the twins, Hamnet and Judith. Unfortunately Hamnet died in 1596 and no one was left to carry on the line.

Nothing much is known about his married life, but as these dates make clear, he was already a married man with a wife and three children to support by the time he was barely twenty-one. Some way of earning a living had to be found, and there are many stories of the different kinds of jobs he is supposed to have have done at this time. It is said that he was teaching at a school near Stratford and it was also possible that he was acting in a theatrical company. One particular anecdote is generally accepted. This legend tells how Shakespeare, together with a few other young men, stole a deer from the park of Sir Thomas Lucy. He was caught and put into prison. Perhaps this incident contributed towards his decision to leave his native village and come to London, in 1586.

He came to London probably in 1586 and how he spent the next six years is not known. Many stories have been in circulation about what have become known as the 'dark years'. Perhaps he had obtained a job as an assistant to the prompter at the theatre or perhaps he held the horses of the noblemen who used to come to the theatre. He, it is known, came into contact with one Richard Field, a fellow Stratfordian who had become a well-established printer in London. It was this man who published *Venus and Adonis* in 1593 and *The Rape of Lucrece* next year.

As the chronological table shows (Chapter 2, *supra*) Shakespeare and Marlowe were born in the same year. It is known that they reached London at almost the same time. This time, the 1580s, was a glorious one for Elizabethan England. Much of the pioneering work in the field of Literature was being done at this time. Sir Philip Sidney was composing the first sequence of love sonnets in English, *Astrophel and*

Stella and Spenser was writing *The Faerie Queene* in Ireland. Young men from all over the country, specially the talented ones, were converging upon London, which was the cultural centre of the time. Lyly had already produced his famous *Euphues* and was trying his hand at drama. Two comedies of his had already been performed before the Queen. By this time the University Wits, Robert Greene, Thomas Nashe and Thomas Kyd had all arrived at London. Marlowe's *Tamburlaine* took the stage by storm in 1587. Experimentations and expansions were going on in every field. As F.E. Halliday describes:

> It was a proud, mercurial, quarrelsome vivid society, a mediaeval people magically vitalised by contact with the Renaissance, quivering with energy.[4]

Shakespeare flung himself heart and soul into this whirlpool and slowly started making a name for himself. Professional jealousy was not wanting and it is to this ignoble sentiment that we owe the first mention of his name. This famous reference occurs in an otherwise unremarkable work by Greene. This pamphlet is entitled *Greene's Groatsworth of wit bought with a Million of Repentances*. This pamphlet (1592) contains a letter addressed to his friends Marlowe, Nashe and Peele. Greene tells his friends to avoid actors:

> Yes, trust them not: for there is an upstart crow, beautified with our feathers that with his Tyger's heart wrapt in a player's hyde, supposes he is as well able to bombast out a blank verse as the best of you: and being an absolute Johannes fac totum, is in his own conceit the only Shake-scene in a country.[5]

There are two clear references to Shakespeare here. Firstly there is the name Shake-scene and secondly the line "Tyger's heart wrapt in a Player's hyde" refers obliquely to Shakespeare's own "O tiger's heart wrapped in a woman's hide" in *Henry VI, Part III*. The remark is malicious but the fact that the well-established University Wits were suffering from jealousy is an indication of Shakespeare's rise to fame and his growing importance in the theatrical world.

These early years, now known as his years of apprenticeship, were highly productive. The two narrative poems *Venus and Adonis* and *The Rape of Lucrece* as well as the sonnets to Mr. W.H. were written at this time. The *Henry VI* trilogy, *Richard III, Titus Andronicus, The Comedy of Errors, The Two Gentlemen of Verona* and *The Taming of the Shrew* are all products of this time. *Titus Andronicus,* which today is not considered to be one of his good plays, was highly popular and had been performed by the three best theatrical companies of the time, patronised by the Earls of Derby, Pembroke and Sussex. If one considers the list of all the plays written at this time, another thing becomes clear, Kyd and Marlowe could write only tragedies, but Shakespeare, even at this early stage, could write history plays, tragedies and comedies successfully. Whether as a lyricist, sonneteer or dramatist, Shakespeare had no rival by 1594.

One of the most popular theatrical companies of this time was the group known as the Lord Chamberlain's Men. Shakespeare had become one of the most important members of this group. He was the writer of the group and every group depended on its writer not only for its popularity, but for its very survival. Shakespeare, till the day of his retirement, stayed with this group and wrote plays only for this company, though its name changed later.

Shakespeare had become a highly successful young man by the time he was twenty-eight. He came to Stratford to find his children grown up and his father an old man of sixty. He stayed there for four months and it is conjectured that both *Venus and Adonis* and *Richard III* were written during this stay here.

This is the time that he came to meet Henry Wriothesley, the Earl of Southampton. He was a handsome aristocrat, almost ten years younger than Shakespeare and a patron of the arts. Shakespeare dedicated both *Venus and Adonis* and *The Rape of Lucrece* to him. The intense love that Shakespeare developed for this earl is expressed not only in "the sugred sonets" he wrote, but in the dedication to these poems as well. The *Dedication* to the later poem says:

> The love I dedicate to your Lordship is without end.... What I have done is yours, what I have to do is yours, being part in all I have devoted yours.[6]

Every word in it rings with authentic love and the words are no mere eulogies of a sycophant to a wealthy patron. The sonnets themselves have recorded this love in more detail. This love was definitely one of the most intense experiences in his life. However, there is a dispute still unsettled about the identity of W.H. There are as many as five contestants to the position.

In those days it was necessary for a poet to be under the patronage of an influential person. The Earl's patronage gave Shakespeare a security that he needed in order to be able to write. His fellow poets were not in an enviable condition. Marlowe met with an untimely and violent death, and Greene died in great poverty. In comparison, our poet was affluent, for he was buying property. A.L. Rowse has given an account of the situation and observed:

> It meant all the difference between the dreadful insecurity poor Greene and others had died of, and having firm ground under his (Shakespeare's) feet.[7]

All this signifies that now, for Shakespeare, the worst was over as far as the financial situation was concerned. He now had a secure and prosperous time to look forward to. With the help of the Earl (as his biographers think) he bought a share in his own company. His company was the foremost one in London and apart from public performances at court, which brought him honour. This is not surprising actually, for it was Shakespeare's plays which brought this honour and prosperity. At this time no other company had a good writer for it. Shakespeare was the only dramatist to have survived the Plague. Kyd was already dead and Peele would die in a few years. Lyly and Lodge had stopped writing plays and Nashe was drawn towards the writing of pamphlets. Marlowe, who could have been his most serious rival, was also dead. Ben Jonson was the only one whose genius equalled Shakespeare's but he had not yet started writing. For the time being, Shakespeare's star was at the zenith.

The light-hearted entertainments that his early comedies offered was just what the audience wanted. *Love's Labour's Lost, A Midsummer Night's Dream* and *The Merchant of Venice* held the audience entranced. Shakespeare, a man of thirty by now, had become a favourite of the educated young men of London. Henry Willoughby, an Oxford undergraduate, writes:

> Yet Tarquin plucked his glistering grape
> And Shakespeare paints poor Lucrece's rape.[8]

In 1597 he was back at Stratford, perhaps writing *King John* when the death of Hamnet, his only son, occurred. No one was left to carry on the line.

His father had, some years ago, applied to the Herald's College for the granting of a coat-of-arms. This would give the family the status of landed gentry which was of great value at the time. Shakespeare now pursued the matter and the request was granted. So when he came back to London it was as a gentleman. He had also bought New Place, which was the second best house in Stratford.

Francis Meres, in his *Palladis Tamia* written in 1598, gives a list of Shakespeare's plays and praises him as the best dramatist of the time:

> As Plautus and Seneca are accounted the best for Comedy and Tragedy among the Latines: so Shakespeare among the English is the most excellent in both kinds for the stage.[9]

This work gives a list of eleven plays besides the two narrative poems and the sonnets.

More recognition came when King James acceded to the throne and extended his patronage to Shakespeare's company. It now became known as the King's Men, which was the highest honour to be had. Many records of this time of his life exist and give a picture of a highly prosperous, popular and creative person.

In 1603 there was another outbreak of plague in London and Shakespeare went down to Stratford. The four great tragedies were being written at this time. *Hamlet* is the last of his Elizabethan plays. *Othello* was performed in King James's court, in 1604. *King Lear* and *Macbeth* were performed in 1606. These, however, were not the only plays he wrote during this time, for the Problem comedies and the Chronicle plays were also being written and performed. The first decade of the Jacobean Age marks a sombre development in his works:

> The Jacobean poetry...is one of compression and lacks the definition of the Elizabethan; thought is packed tight and imagery reduced to the single word of metaphors.[10]

The year 1608 was one that brought both sorrow and joy to Shakespeare. His mother passed away and his first grandchild was born. Shakespeare now started writing his last Romances. His sonnets, which had been in circulation in manuscript for some time, were published in 1609. He retired from his company in 1611 and settled in his native village. *The Winter's Tale* was staged this year.

Shakespeare continued coming to London and his name occurs in many documents. A royal betrothal in 1612 was the occasion for the staging of *The Tempest*. It is said that Shakespeare himself played the role of Prospero.

His days, however, were drawing to a close, and in Jan. 1616 his last will and testament was drawn up. A few months later, on April 23rd, his supposed birthday, he breathed his last. There is an elaborate tomb on his grave with many allegorical figures and inscriptions. The most famous of the inscriptions is a quatrain, supposed to have been written by the poet himself:

> Good friend, for Jesus sake forbeare
> To dig the dust enclosed here!
> Blest be the man yt spares the stones.
> And curst be he yt moves my bones.[11]

(b) Shakespeare's Works

It has not been always possible to get the right dates of the compositions of his works. Henslowe used to make entries in his *Diary* of the performances of the plays and there are entries in the *Stationer's Register* as well. Modern critics have agreed on the following dates:

Phase I

1591	–	*The Comedy of Errors.*
'92	–	*The Two Gentlemen of Verona, Henry VI, Parts I-III.*
'93	–	*Richard III, Romeo and Juliet, Venus and Adonis.*

Phase II

1594	–	*The Rape of Lucrece,* The Sonnets, *Titus Andronicus, King Richard II, A Midsummer Night's Dream. Love's Labour's Lost, The Taming of the Shrew, King John.*
'95	–	*The Merchant of Venice.*
'97	–	*Henry IV, Part I.*
'98	–	*Henry IV, Part II, The Merry Wives of Windsor.*
'99	–	*King Henry V, Much Ado About Nothing, Julius Caesar.*
1600	–	*As You Like It, Twelfth Night.*

Phase III

1602	–	*Hamlet, Troilus and Cressida, All's well that Ends well.*
'04	–	*Measure for Measure, Othello.*
'05	–	*King Lear.*
'06	–	*Macbeth.*
'07	–	*Antony and Cleopatra.*
'08	–	*Coriolanus, Timon of Athens, Pericles.*

Phase IV

1610	–	*Cymbeline, The Winter's Tale, The Tempest*
'11	–	*Henry VIII.*

Shakespeare's dramatic career has been divided into four phases as given above. The first phase, that of Experiment, goes on till 1594 and according to some can be taken to have continued till '95. At this time he was mostly re-writing plays that already existed. His style had not developed yet and there are many traces of immaturity. Yet there is a richness in his poetry at this time which is lacking in the later works. Much ornamentation and word-play is there. The characters, also, are inexpertly drawn.

The second phase stretching from 1595 to 1601 is of development. He now has the patronage of the Earl of Southampton which has secured his future, and now he can devote himself to perfecting his art. Having by this time mastered the technique of the blank verse, he could modulate it to suit each character. Consequently the characters become better drawn, with evidences of psychological insight. The plots too become more skilfully managed, as the adaptations he made in the chronicle plays and the golden comedies show.

The third phase introduces a change. The prevailing mood is sombre and gloomy. The frailties of human nature, the inevitable presence of evil—these now trouble his spirit. Even the comedies written during this period are gloomy ones, as the very name 'Dark Comedies' shows. The four great tragedies reflect the dominant mood.

The last phase, known as the Romance period, shows peace and tranquillity. A mature wisdom that accepts the presence of evil along with the good predominates. No other play shows this better than the one that is going to be studied—*The Tempest,* which is his last complete work.

(c) Notes on Individual Works

The Comedy of Errors

This is now generally taken to be his first play. It is definitely the shortest. A well-known comedy of Plautus, popular at the time, *Menaechmi*, provides the plot. Shakespeare has altered the plot a little for he has introduced two pairs of twins where there is but one in Plautus. The complexities proceeding from mistaken identities have naturally become much greater. It was presented at Court in 1594, but had possibly been performed earlier.

The Two Gentlemen of Verona

This play is also thought to be Shakespeare's first. While this is disputed, it is definitely the first of his romantic comedies. Two pairs of lovers, two servants and two fathers provide a well-balanced group of *dramatis personae* and this makes for a symmetrical plot. The theme of friendship and love in conflict is presented with skill and the stress falls on the former. The theme of forgiveness and reconciliation, a theme that runs through the whole of his works to culminate in *The Tempest*, makes its first appearance in this play. Lance the clown is the forerunner of many others.

Henry VI, Parts 1, 2 and 3

Shakespeare stands alone in his creation of these colourful and patriotic Chronicle plays. He takes up the serious issues of kingship and its duties, the relationship between the king and the subject and the fascinating subject of the personality of the king.

Holinshed's *Chronicles* provided the material for all his history plays. This trilogy, staged in 1592, was so popular that the entire cycle was performed three times in eight days. He presents a blood-thirsty world of betrayal and conflict and ends with regicide. In spite of all this, the trilogy evokes national pride and patriotism. Its poetry has a lot of bombast in it and it was to a line in this play, "O tiger's heart wrapped in a woman's hide" that Greene had referred to, slightly rewording it, in a disparaging and jealous spirit.

Richard III

This can be regarded as more a tragedy than a history play. As it is the *Henry VI* trilogy shows Marlowe's influence in its poetry and the influence extends to this play also, for the hero, King Richard III, is a Marlovian figure though he is far more complex as a Machiavellian villain. After *Hamlet* this is the second longest play of Shakespeare.

Romeo and Juliet

This is the first of his romantic tragedies and tells the story of family feuds and of star-crossed lovers. The well-known maxim "character is destiny" is not borne out by this play for here it is Fate that dominates the action. He follows the original story quite closely in the play. Already his power of versification is making itself felt and the character of Mercutio is a piece of original invention.

Venus and Adonis

Based on Greek myths, this is a long narrative poem—a form that was very popular in his day. The poem became very popular, and ran through ten or eleven editions. Here he shows a new facet of his versatile genius. The poem is in sextains, *i.e.*, a quatrain followed by a couplet, and Shakespeare evinces total mastery of this form. This was a completely new field for him, but he had many models to guide him. Many such narrative poems were being written at this time and Shakespeare shows that he is as much at home in the telling of a sensuous love-story in a lyrical form as he is in drama.

The Rape of Lucrece

This is the second of his narrative poems based on classical myths. Like *Venus and Adonis* this too was dedicated to the Earl of Southampton. The poem is in rhyme royal, a complex stanza of seven lines, and Shakespeare shows great expertise in it. Tarquin the hero of the poem, is a tragic figure in the complexity evident in his character. The psychological insight evinced in his portrayal raises the poem far above that of a mere well-written story.

The Sonnets

Though the Earl of Southampton has been nowhere named yet he is, generally, supposed to be "the onlie begetter" to whom the sequence has been dedicated. It is a sequence of one hundred and fifty-four sonnets, the majority of which is addressed to Mr. W.H. and the rest to the equally mysterious Dark Lady. It is thought that the initials Mr. W.H. are an inverted form of Henry Wriothesley, which was the name of the Earl of Southampton. The other candidates nominated by the critics are: (1) William Warbart, (2) William Hare, (3) William Harry, (4) William Hathaway, (5) William Henry. The intensity of love that can be easily seen breathing through every line makes this sonnet-sequence unique among those produced at this time.

Titus Andronicus

This is a typical blood-and-thunder tragedy that appealed to the Elizabethan audience but does not appeal to our modern tastes. Shakespeare looked to Kyd's *The Spanish Tragedy* for a model as far as the structure and the theme are concerned. This play also contains a parody of a very well-known passage of Kyd, beginning "O eyes no eyes but fountains full of tears."

Richard II

Shakespeare's plays are universal rather than topical, yet this play is more topical than many others. Queen Elizabeth's angry exclamation on seeing the play is well known. "I am Richard II, know ye that?"... The deposition of the king was a highly sensitive issue and all the scenes dealing with this event had to be omitted when the play was staged. Critics are of the opinion that in this historical tragedy the hero King Richard II is a study in weakness.

A Midsummer Night's Dream

This fantasy, as the name proclaims, is one of his best early works. It is a fairy-tale romance in which fairies take an active part and influence human actions. It has been said that Shakespeare, in this play, created this new genre and he will be using it again in *The Tempest*. The characterization of this play is specially important as three levels of characters have been presented: the fairies, the pair of romantic lovers and the robust, earthy villagers. Among the last, Bottom has become immortal.

Love's Labour's Lost

In this play Shakespeare deals with characters who are mostly royal and courtly, though some humbler ones are also present. The dialogue is full of sparkling wit. One of the passages of this play has become particularly well known. Lord Berowne, the merriest and the wittiest of the lords, who is also supposed to be slightly autobiographical, denounces ornate and witty diction and vows to turn to simplicity.

The Taming of the Shrew

This play, performed in 1594, is in an Italian setting. The two main characters, Kate the shrew of the title and Petruchio the tamer, have both been effectively portrayed. The theme is the conflict between husband and wife for supremacy. It is a play providing boisterous enjoyment.

King John

This is an entirely historical play, yet it has a topical quality as well. Religion is an important issue just as it was in Elizabeth's days. Like Queen Elizabeth, King John also carried on a lifelong struggle with the Pope. Religion, though important, is not the central theme and the play cannot be called a religious play. It is essentially a patriotic play and relationship with foreign powers is the theme.

The Merchant of Venice

This play ushers in the group of the four happy or golden comedies. Though the play is named after Antonio, yet he is not the most important character in it. The position is taken by Shylock the Jew, who is a class by himself. Portia the heroine is one of the most charming personalities of Shakespeare. The Elizabethan plays made numerous and effective use of disguises and Shakespeare has used this convention in this play. There are three female characters in it and all of them put on male disguises. Shakespeare's versification has matured to a remarkable extent and the play contains some fine passages.

Henry IV, Parts 1 and 2

English history plays reached a high peak of excellence in these two plays. Falstaff remains unsurpassed as a comic character. Shakespeare's own Sir Toby of *Twelfth Night* seems to be a paler version. The rejection of Falstaff by King Henry V remains one of the most moving scenes of Shakespeare. The play is about the duties and responsibilities of kings and the second part emphasizes this theme. Yet the Falstaff scenes in the first part are so fine that they are the ones which are remembered and the serious ones are forgotten, though they are psychologically interesting.

The Merry Wives of Windsor

Queen Elizabeth had been so captivated by Falstaff that she ordered a play to be written depicting "the fat knight in love", and this play was the result. It begins where the second part of *Henry IV* ends. By this time Ben Jonson had started writing and it is thought that Corporal Nym of this play is a parody of a humour character.

King Henry V

This play presents Shakespeare's concept of the ideal king. The twin themes of patriotism and of the responsibilities of kingship dominate the play. The famous battle of Agincourt is presented in a thoroughly impartial manner. On one side there is heroism and nobility and on the other cruelty and bloodshed. Shakespeare depicts the young king as the ideal leader of men in the field of battle and later as the ideal administrator, tempering justice with mercy.

Much Ado About Nothing

This belongs to the group of the golden comedies, treating, like all of them, the theme of love. This theme is presented in many different ways. Physical love based on outer appearance is found in the Hero-Claudio plot, rejection of married love is presented through Benedick and Beatrice and the theme of love versus friendship is also given importance. Shakespeare shows mature artistry in managing the plot as well, with a clear-cut main plot and a subsidiary plot.

Julius Caesar

This is categorised as a Roman tragedy and is followed by another, *Antony and Cleopatra.* It is an entirely political play and the conflict between tyranny and liberty is the central theme. The Forum scene is one of the best in Shakespeare. The story is taken from Lord North's translation of Plutarch's *Lives*. It was highly successful on the stage.

As You Like It

This is the sunniest of the golden comedies. The major part of the play takes place in pastoral surroundings and therefore it is also called a pastoral comedy. Love is the central theme, presented in four different ways through four pairs of lovers. These comprise royal characters as well as humble shepherds. All are neatly paired off at the end and there are no less than four marriages. Courtly love is found in Rosalind and Orlando and a more domestic love in the shepherds. Rosalind, one of his most captivating heroines, uses the disguise of a shepherd and this produces some of the most effective instances of dramatic irony.

Twelfth Night

This is the last of the golden comedies. Here too the main theme is love and two different aspects of this theme have been presented. This play contains the Falstaff-like character of Sir Toby and one of Shakespeare's most famous jesters, Feste. It also presents one of his rare "humour" characters in Malvolio the melancholy Puritan. Viola the heroine, remains in the disguise of a page-boy in all but one scene, which is the longest duration that any of his heroines spends in disguise.

Hamlet

This is the first of his four Great Tragedies and the last of the plays written during the reign of Queen Elizabeth. The character of Hamlet has gained so much importance that the fact that it is essentially a revenge tragedy is often overlooked. The play follows the pattern of the usual blood-and-thunder revenge tragedy of Kyd but Shakespeare has given the play so much polished sophistication and psychological complexity that it has left the limitations of the revenge tragedy far behind it and blazed a new path.

Troilus and Cressida

The first of the problem comedies or the dark comedies, Shakespeare goes back to ancient Greece in this play. All these plays are concerned with the problem of evil as the tragedies are, but these do not end tragically. The atmosphere, however, is so steeped in gloom that these have come to be known as the problem comedies. There is a speech by Ulysses, the degree-speech, which has become specially well known. It has been thought that Ulysses's speeches echo the poet's own thoughts.

All's Well that Ends Well

Like *Troilus and Cressida* this play, too, belongs to the group of the problem comedies, though it is less satirical. The conflict between virtue and nobility is expounded in the main plot of Bertram and Helena. Besides this, there are many sub-themes. The difference in attitude is clearly seen in the character of Parolles the braggart soldier which is a purely satirical portrait, totally different from the lovable Falstaff.

Measure for Measure

This is the third of the problem comedies. It is a very bitter play, yet, in one respect it resembles *As You Like It* the happiest of the golden comedies. In both the plays there are four marriages at the end but the atmosphere is entirely different in each. Shakespeare has taken up, among other things, the theme of justice which is one of the main issues in these later and more serious plays.

Othello

This has been called the *Romeo and Juliet* of the later Shakespeare, and is usually taken to be the first of the plays written in the Jacobean era. In Othello the hero we have a study in the emotion of jealousy, to be paralleled later in the character of Leontes in *The Winter's Tale.* It gives us the enigmatic figure of Iago the malcontent who brings about the tragic murder of Desdemona out of no discernible motive. Coleridge's phrase "motiveless malignity" with reference to Iago has become famous in Shakespeare tragedy criticism. The play is a villain tragedy and also a domestic tragedy.

King Lear

This play is thought to be his greatest and has been called a cosmic drama. Shakespeare has given sublimity to a primitive story that is rather like a fairytale. The character of the Fool is a unique one even among the Fools of Shakespeare. The scene of Cordelia's death is so moving that Dr. Johnson had said that he could not bear to read it. The heath-scene is one of the most moving scenes in Shakespeare. Judged by any standard, it is one of the greatest tragedies.

Macbeth

The fourth of the four great tragedies, this is taken to be his gloomiest play. He takes up a story from the history of Scotland, intending it as a compliment to the Scottish King. Tragedies are hero-centred plays, but in this tragedy he has created a female character who has no parallel in drama—the forceful figure of Lady Macbeth. Shakespeare makes use of three witches in this play whose prophecies mislead the hero, and Lady Macbeth has been grouped with them and is sometimes called the Fourth Witch of the play.

Antony and Cleopatra

Shakespeare goes back to Roman history once more, as he did for the plot of *Julius Caesar*, and writes this tragedy as a sequel to that play. This play shows the fortunes of Mark Antony after the battle at Philippi. He goes to Egypt which had fallen to his share as a member of the Triumvirate. There he meets Cleopatra and so the theme of love is introduced. The play shows the all-compensating power of love for which all losses can be faced and welcomed.

Coriolanus

This is a Roman tragedy and a political one as well. Shakespeare shows in his hero a man of such nobility that he cannot stoop to court the populace. He is intolerant of meanness and vulgarity and cannot disguise his contempt for the mob. In a social structure where popular support is needed such an attitude leads to tragic doom and Coriolanus is punished for his obstinacy.

Timon of Athens

Una Ellis-Fermor had proved that this is an unfinished work, and it is known that it was never staged. The end shows the hero's withdrawal from society and that gives the play the sense of an ending.

Pericles

This play marks the beginning of his last phase. The theme of sin and repentance leading to forgiveness and regeneration is the theme of all these last romances and it has been worked out in this play as well. The same themes will recur, with variations, in the next three plays.

Cymbeline

This is the second of the four last Romances and repeats the same theme as found in *Pericles*. The heroine Imogen is the last of the Shakespearean heroines to don a disguise. King Cymbeline loses his children as Pericles does and finds them back after long years of separation. The same atmosphere of fulfilment is found at the end as in *Pericles*.

The Winter's Tale

Like *Othello*, this is a study in jealousy and, in addition, it has all the important features of the last Romances. This play is the most notorious example of the violation of the classical unities that Shakespeare affords, for it covers sixteen years and spreads over different countries. The theme of sin and repentance and forgiveness is repeated here as in all the last romances. Not only does the supposedly dead Queen Hermione come to life but the abandoned daughter of King Leontes is also restored to him.

Henry VIII

This is not just another chronicle play for it discusses a definite central theme—patience in adversity. The King as well as the other characters are taught this lesson. It ends, like the romances, with the continuance of a purer life.

The Two Noble Kinsmen

This play was written in collaboration with Fletcher, and tells the story of Palamon and Arcite as given by Chaucer in his *The Knight's Tale*. Shakespeare wrote the major parts of Act I, parts of Act III and Act V. Fletcher, however, introduced a vulgar sub-plot and Shakespeare did not collaborate with him any further.

REFERENCES

1. Ribner, Irving, *William Shakespeare: Life, Times and Theatre*. London: John Wiley & Sons Inc., 1969, p. 31.
2. Cited in Halliday, F.E., *The Life of Shakespeare*. London: Gerald Duckworth & Co. Ltd., 1961, p. 20.

3. Ribner, I., *op. cit.*, p. 38.
4. Halliday, *op. cit.*, p. 59.
5. Quoted in Ribner, *op. cit.*, p. 45.
6. Quoted in Halliday, *op. cit.*, pp. 102-03.
7. Rowse, A.L., *William Shakespeare: A Biography*. London: Macmillan & Co. Ltd., 1963, p. 201.
8. Halliday, *op. cit.*, p. 118.
9. *Ibid.*, p. 138.
10. *Ibid.*, p. 183.
11. Quoted in Ribner, I., *op. cit.*, p. 64.

4

A Brief Outline of the Story

(a) The Story of *The Tempest*

The story of *The Tempest,* as it is presented on the stage, actually starts some twelve years earlier. At that time Prospero who is the hero of the play was the Duke of Milan, that is, its sovereign ruler. He was better fitted for an intellectual life than an administrative one, for he loved to study. He took no interest in ruling his kingdom but immersed himself in intellectual pursuits and left the governing of the kingdom in the hands of his brother.

He had, thus, made two mistakes at this stage of his life. He neglected his duties towards his subjects, and, in entrusting the ruling of the kingdom to Antonio, placed almost irresistible temptation in front of his brother. This was a bit unfair to everyone—his subjects as well as his brother.

The brother, Antonio, was not only ambitious, but treacherous as well. Taking the help of the King of Naples, he usurped the kingdom but dared not kill Prospero because of his popularity which might lead to popular uprising. Instead he thought of a devilish plan for killing Prospero slowly but inevitably in such a way that no one will ever know. He placed Prospero and his baby daughter Miranda—at that time barely three years old—in an old boat, and set them adrift on the sea:

> they prepared
> A rotten carcass of a butt, not rigged,
> Nor tackle, sail nor mast—the very rats
> Instinctively have quit it.[1]

A loyal and kindly courtier Gonzalo, had put provisions, clothes, etc. in the boat. Most important of all, he had put books of magic on board as well. Prospero, along with his baby daughter, reached "by divine providence" the island in which he has been living for the last twelve years.

Miranda had been ignorant of all these happenings. Now, when the play opens it seems to Prospero that because of certain concatenation of circumstances, the time has come for him to acquaint her with this past history. He reveals all this to her and thus the audience is also told about them. Miranda had only a dim memory of the past.

Prospero had attained mastery over the magical arts and when he arrived at this unnamed and unidentified island, he found the place inhabited only by supernatural spirits, apart from ordinary animals. This island had a sinister history up till then for a witch named Sycorax had been banished there. She gave birth to a monster Caliban and, enraged with Ariel who was an airy spirit, had imprisoned him within a tree. She had died without setting him free. Prospero, on arrival, freed him and Ariel became his servant thereafter. Caliban was a monster and incapable of either learning or of gratitude. Though Prospero tried to educate and civilize him, the efforts went in vain and Caliban developed into a vengeful creature, hating his benefactor but forced to obey him.

This is the situation when the play opens. Now Prospero, after twelve years of repentance and suffering, has attained great mental placidity and wants to bring his present condition to an end. He also aims at enabling Miranda to lead a normal life among other human beings in a normal society. Her condition is unique. She has never seen any human being other than her father for the island does not have anyone in it but for Caliban who is not fully human, and spirits. A return to normal life is seen as desirable. This is not merely the normal desire of a man to be among men. That would be natural and realistic and gives his characters and everything else a far more serious dimension. Prospero knows that his brother is guilty of treachery and intended murder (for he had tried to kill Prospero and Miranda, however indirectly). He must be made to repent, for the good of his own soul. Prospero also must forgive and be reconciled to him. The issues of sin, repentance, forgiveness and reconciliation are serious issues that have given a religious dimension to all the last romances. Shakespeare, with infinite artistry, has contrived a plot which brings together these serious issues and Prospero, in addition, returns to a normal society.

With this intent, therefore, Prospero, with the help of Ariel, causes a tempest in the sea. A ship, containing, besides others, the two characters who have been guilty of ill-treating. Prospero, gets caught in this tempest and is wrecked. Prospero had known about the ship passing near the island and had caused the storm. This shipwreck is only an apparent one and not real. Prospero had directed Ariel to manage things in such a way that the ship would not be harmed. The characters, too, are all saved. They reach separate parts of the island alone or in groups. Thus Ferdinand, son of Alonso the King of Naples, reaches the island alone and believes himself to be the only survivor. The other characters also reach the island at a different point and believe Ferdinand to be dead, to Alonso's great sorrow.

Ferdinand is met by Ariel who remains invisible to him and leads him to Prospero and Miranda by singing songs. Music plays a very important part in this play. Here these two songs, of which the famous "full fathom five" is one, leads him to Prospero, for Ferdinand cannot see Ariel and he follows the song that Ariel sings.

When Ferdinand does reach Prospero, Miranda sees a young man for the first time and cannot believe that he is a human being and not a spirit. She falls deeply in love with him, and this love is reciprocated by Ferdinand. This is exactly what Prospero had wanted but he hides his satisfaction and behaves with imperious rudeness to Ferdinand, making it clear to him that he is only a servant. This is merely to try Ferdinand and see how true his love is. The young couple pass the test, Prospero is convinced of the strength and endurance of their love for each other and blesses them:

All thy vexations
Were but my trials of thy love, and thou
Hast strangely stood the test. Here, afore heaven,
I ratify this my rich gift.[2]

It is far otherwise among the other men of the ship. Instead of solidarity, there is treachery and discontent. The noble characters, Antonio and Sebastian, do not present themselves in a light that inspires admiration. Alonso, believing his only son Ferdinand to be dead, is overwhelmed with grief and is distractedly looking for him, but Antonio and Sebastian, far from sympathising with him and consoling him, are conspiring against him. Antonio had at one time overthrown his own brother and brought his own native land under foreign domination by conspiring with Alonso. Once a traitor, always a traitor, and he now conspires with Sebastian to overthrow Alonso. They plan to kill Alonso when he is sleeping but Prospero averts this disaster by making Ariel wake Gonzalo just on time.

There is another group, the group of comic characters, comprising two clowns, Stephano and Trinculo. These two excite the admiration of Caliban, who takes them for gods and swears allegiance to them. These three then hatch a plot against Prospero. This is a parody of the plot against Alonso by Antonio and Sebastian. Such comic parodies of the serious action are often to be found in these plays. This plot, too, is foiled by Prospero's watchfulness.

Finally Prospero, in order to instil a sense of the seriousness of their crime into the men who had wronged him twelve years ago and bring them to repentance, makes Ariel appear as a harpy and spoil a banquet that had been laid out for them. Ariel, then, in a condemnatory speech makes them conscious of the heinousness of their crime. This has the desired effect, for both Alonso and the other culprit Antonio, are overcome with repentance and fear, respectively. They are all brought to Prospero's cave, after having been put in a state of hypnotic entrancement.

By this time the two young lovers have formally plighted their troth, and a masque has been presented to celebrate the occasion. Such masques were very popular at the time. The royal characters see them sitting, playing chess. Ferdinand and Miranda, too, see them and Miranda speaks the memorable, oft-quoted lines:

> O wonder!
> How many goodly creatures are there here!
> How beauteous mankind is! O brave new world
> That has such people in't.[3]

The culprits also see Prospero. Alonso is truly penitent, but it is doubtful whether Antonio and Sebastian are. Prospero is now above all mean thoughts of revenge. He reproves them with calm dignity and forgives his brother.

The play thus ends happily. We see Prospero getting his dukedom back, Ferdinand and Miranda are united and their union also unites the two kingdoms of Milan and Naples.

Prospero, however, realises that his magical powers should play no part in the life he is going to lead as the ruler of Milan. So, before he meets the culprits and forgives them, he renounces his magical powers. In a solemn scene he calls all the creatures of the island to witness the powers of his magic and his renunciation of it:

> I'll break my staff
> Bury it certain fathoms in the earth
> And deeper than did ever plummet sound
> I'll drown my book.[4]

It is only after he has divested himself of his supernatural powers that he meets the other characters and forgives them. At the end there is an epilogue spoken by Prospero which looks forward to the days in future which he will spend as the Duke of Milan. The enchanted island with its beauty and his supernatural powers will become a memory and the great Prospero will lead the life of a king who is also a hermit:

> ....will retire me to my Milan where
> Every third thought shall be my grave.[5]

(b) The Genre of the Play

The Tempest, along with the other three plays of the last part of Shakespeare's career, has been classified as a romance, which is slightly different from a romantic comedy. As a matter of fact, these last four plays are actually unclassifiable and whatever label is given to them seems to be inadequate. This has led different critics to give different names like: pastoral play, tragi-comedy, pastoral tragi-comedy, etc. The majority of the critics, however, agree to call it a romance. It is necessary, therefore, to know the essential features of romances.

A great wealth and variety of men and action is one of the most important features of romances. The writers of romances are themselves conscious of this fact and they have, down the ages, asserted the need for variety as well as copiousness of characters and events. Thus Tasso in his famous romance *Orlando Furioso* declared:

> To complete the great tapestry on which
> I am working I feel the need for a great
> variety of strands.[6]

This need for variety is ably fulfilled by our play. It has been recognised from the very beginning, for example, that *The Tempest* has more variety of character than any other play of Shakespeare (*vide* Chapter 7, *infra*). We have supernatural characters like Ariel and other spirits. These other spirits do not speak but they are frequently present on the stage, as for example they spread the banquet and dance in the feast-scene; they take the shape of dogs and chase Trinculo, Stephano and Caliban and in the masque two of them as well as Ariel take part. At the end of the masque a whole host of them appear as harvesters and nymphs. Apart from these supernatural characters the world of the sub-human is also covered in the person of Caliban. When we come to the human world we see that the entire social spectrum is presented from royalty to servants. Alonso and his party present the courtly circle and the lower orders are presented by Stephano and Trinculo as well as the ship's crew, of whom the Boatswain is the most important.

As far as the events are concerned, a brief catalogue will make it clear how various the action is: the revenge motive is presented twice—at first in Prospero who says he wants to take revenge on his brother, and then in Caliban's plotting against Prospero's life. Murder is presented in many different ways, though, true to the spirit of romance, actual murder does not take place. Antonio and Sebastian plot the murder of Alonso and Gonzalo and Caliban instigates Stephano to kill Prospero. Romantic love is presented, particularly in the log-bearing scene. Parental and filial love is presented in the relationship between Prospero and Miranda and even more emphatically in that between Alonso and Ferdinand. Thus both in character and in action there is great variety in *The Tempest.*

The element of wonder or fantasy is extremely important for romances. The presence of the supernatural is almost the distinctive feature of romances. In this play the supernatural almost controls the entire action. Prospero's magical powers are supernatural powers and with them he controls Ariel, the leader of a whole host of spirits. He controls the entire action of the play in this manner. In no other play except *A Mid-summer Night's Dream* does the supernatural play as active a role as in this play.

Quest motif is also an important feature of the romance. This is particularly to be found in mediaeval Arthurian romances. This involves separation, overcoming of obstacles, and other adventures. In this play the motif of the quest is presented in many ways, at its simplest in the trial of Ferdinand. He has to overcome the obstacle of demeaning physical labour in order to deserve the love of Miranda and be united to her. In addition to this there are: (a) the quest of Alonso and the courtiers in their search of Ferdinand, (b) Ariel's quest for freedom, (c) Stephano and Trinculo's ridiculous quest for glory, paralleled by, (d) Antonio's and Sebastian's quest for power, and (e) Prospero's quest for his usurped dukedom.

In addition to these there are several other less important features of romance which are to be found in our play, like separation of the hero and the heroine, conflict with the villain, the return and recognition of lost characters, the trials of the hero, etc. All of these are to be found in *The Tempest* and these justify its label of romance.

It has also been called a pastoral play. The two themes of Art and Nature are juxtaposed in it (*vide* the section on The Theme of Natural Life, Chapter 6, *infra*). Frank Kermode analyses how Prospero represents Art as Caliban represents Nature. According to this critic Art is shown as contrasting Nature. This is a complex aspect of the play. Prospero's power is a benevolent power and this power has rid the island of Sycorax the evil witch and turned the island into a place where there is peace and harmony in the lap of nature. Aspects of nature like the flora and the fauna are repeatedly mentioned. J.P. Cutts observes:

> The island governed by the benevolent powers of Prospero is in itself a type of the golden age island where no ill is ultimately allowed.[7]

The play has been viewed as a tragi-comedy as well. By this time, that is, the beginning of the seventeenth century, tragi-comedies had come into fashion and were highly popular. Writers like Beaumont and Fletcher were producing one popular tragi-comedy after another and Shakespeare's own plays, the four romances, became very popular. Fletcher has given a famous description of tragi-comedy:

> A tragi-comedy is not so-called in respect of mirth and killings, but in respect it wants death, which is enough to make it no tragedy, yet bringing some one near to it, which is enough to make it no comedy.[8]

This is perfectly illustrated by *The Tempest* for in it Alonso and Gonzalo are brought near death. Alonso believes Ferdinand to be dead and Ferdinand believes Alonso to be so. All those in the ship are also brought near death. No one, however, does really die; we have a marriage instead. We have hopes of a better future through the continuity of life in the younger generation.

There is also the view that interprets *The Tempest* not as a play, but as a dramatic poem. Thus, after analysing many phrases, metaphors and images in the play, R.A. Brower comes to the conclusion that the play emphasizes transformations of many different kinds at many different levels, the key-metaphor of the play being "sea-change" in Ariel's famous song "Full fathom five". This change or transformation comes over everything, the island is a place where everything may become something else. Everyone in the play undergoes a change. Prospero changes from a negligent ruler into a dutiful father and a wise mage. Miranda changes from a girl into a woman, Ferdinand changes from a young carefree prince to a chivalrous knight ready to shoulder any burdens for the sake of his lady. Alonso changes from a wrong-doer into a repentant sovereign. These and many other changes take place and the critic comes to the conclusion that the play is a poem:

> Thus *The Tempest* is, like Marvell's "Garden", a Metaphysical poem of metamorphoses.[9]

REFERENCES

1. Gill, R., ed., *The Tempest,* Act I, sc. ii, lines 145-48, p. 10. Oxford, The University Press, 1998. All the quotations from this play will be from this edn.
2. Act IV, sc. i, *ll.* 5-8, p. 63.
3. Act V, sc. i, *ll.* 181-84, p. 82.
4. Act V, sc. i, *ll.* 54-57, p. 77.
5. Act V, sc. i, *ll.* 310-11, p. 87.
6. Waldman, G., transl., *Orlando Furioso*, Oxford, The University Press, 1974; 13: 81-82.
7. Cutts, John P., *Music and the Supernatural in The Tempest*, in Palmer, D.J., ed., *Shakespeare: The Tempest,* Casebook series. Macmillan, 1968, p. 196.
8. Quoted in Champion, L.S., *The Evolution of Shakespeare's Comedy: A Study in Dramatic Perspective*. Harvard Univ. Press, 1970, p. 184.
9. Brower, R.A., *The Mirror of Analogy,* in Palmer, D.J., *op. cit.*, p. 174.

5

A Scene-wise Critical Analysis

Act I, scene i

This, the first scene of the play, can be treated as the Prologue. Prologues formed an important part of the classical plays, introducing the play and its theme. Many of Shakespeare's plays have Prologues, coming before the real action of the play has started. In most plays, however, the Prologue is not given separately, but incorporated within the play, as is the case with *The Tempest,* where it forms the first scene.

The scene shows a terrible tempest in the sea. The ship in which Alonso the King of Naples, Sebastian his brother, his son Ferdinand and Antonio the Duke of Milan were travelling is caught in the tempest. They are returning from Tunis where they had gone to attend the marriage of the King's daughter, Claribel, and are now caught in the storm.

The scene is a highly realistic one. The Ship-Master, the Boatswain and the other sailors are doing their best to keep the ship afloat. The noble passengers, that is, Alonso, Antonio and others come and talk to the Boatswain. They are only hindering him from doing his work, and the Boatswain makes no secret of the fact:

> You mar our labours. Keep your cabin—
> You do assist the storm.[1]

The waves are no respecters of persons, as he points out. However, though they try their best, they cannot save the ship. It splits and, to the despair of everyone, sinks. Everyone prays to God and as they all believe, are prepared to be drowned. The scene ends in a pious yet realistic sentence by Gonzalo:

> The wills above be done, but I would fain die a dry death.[2]

The scene is a very short one, for the sentence quoted above is the last sentence of the scene, which runs to sixty-six lines. The major part of the scene is in prose. Antonio speaks in verse, for a total of seven lines and so does Gonzalo, when speaking to him, for four lines. Except for these eleven lines the rest of the scene is in prose. This is but to be expected, for the Ship-Master and the Boatswain, who are the chief speakers in the scene, are humble characters as opposed to the king and the courtiers. It is an important feature of the Elizabethan and Jacobean plays that in them the noble characters speak in verse and the humbler characters in prose. Here the same convention has been followed. (For more information see Chapter 11, Poetic Style, *infra.*)

Another point to be noted in this connection is the realistic quality of the scene. Shakespeare gives a convincing picture of the disaster in only sixty-six lines. Most remarkable of all is the manner in which the Boatswain speaks to the noble characters. He is so pre-occupied with struggling against the storm and impending death that he cannot be respectful to them. Nothing conveys the sense of disaster as concretely as his impoliteness:

> You are a councillor; if you can command these elements to silence and work the peace of the present, we will not handle a rope more—use your authority. If you can't, give thanks you have lived so long.[3]

When death stares one in the face, social conventions are forgotten. We shall see the same man in the last scene, when he will inform every one of how the ship is safe and sound and how they were all brought to Prospero's cell. He will then speak in faultless iambic pentametres, but now, facing death, he speaks in prose and in a disrespectful manner. Thus, while making use of prevailing conventions, Shakespeare has brought the seriousness of the storm home to the reader. Coleridge has written an important essay on the first scene.

Act I, scene ii

In this scene there are two main characters, Prospero and Miranda. They are introduced first, and then the others. This is an expository scene, that is, many facts will be explained and much information given in this scene. Prospero is the lord of the island where the entire action takes place and Miranda is his daughter. The island is uninhabited by man and therefore Miranda has never seen any man but her father. Prospero is a great magician and it becomes clear that the tempest described in the first scene had been called up by him, for Miranda says:

> If by your art, my dearest father, you have
> Put the wild waters in this roar, allay them.[4]

Her young and sensitive heart is racked with pity for the drowned sailors, whose sufferings she has seen from the safe distance of the island. Prospero reassures her that the poor mariners have not been harmed at all. He then tells her that the time has come when she should be told about the true nature of themselves.

He then takes off his magic robe. This is a significant action for it is the insignia of his magical powers and when he lays it aside his personality undergoes a subtle change. He is no longer Prospero the mighty magician, but Prospero the father who now sits down with his child to talk to her. He reveals the fact that he was once the Duke of Milan and that Miranda therefore is actually a princess and his heiress, that is, the future Duchess of Milan. Prospero himself, in those days, was more interested in studies than in ruling his kingdom. This being the case, he entrusted the governing of the kingdom to his brother Antonio:

> The government I cast upon my brother
> And to my state grew stranger, being transported
> And rapt in secret studies.[5]

His brother then betrayed him. He conspired with the King of Naples Alonso, promising him homage and tribute if he helped him to overthrow Prospero, thus making him the absolute ruler of Milan. Thus Antonio betrayed not only his brother but his own motherland as well, so that he could become what was, in effect, a puppet-king.

Thus, with the help of Alonso, Antonio deposed Prospero, but dared not kill him on account of his popularity. He then put Prospero and Miranda in a rotten boat and set them adrift without a sail or any other fittings. It was a miracle that they reached this island at all and Prospero highlights this miraculous element by not offering any explanation at all, instead he only says: "By divine providence" when Miranda asks "How came we ashore?" Indeed, God's mercy is beyond human senses.

Surrounded by enemies, Prospero, as he tells Miranda, had one friend who helped them survive. This was Gonzalo. This man had been put in charge of the whole affair and he had put food, water, clothes and other necessaries in the boat. Most important of all, he had also put Prospero's magic books in it.

Miranda now goes back to her first cause of puzzlement—why had Prospero caused this storm at all? Prospero answers that by good fortune his enemies had travelled near the island and he means to take advantage of this fact. How he is going to do so he does not explain, for Miranda falls asleep. The sleep is perhaps caused by Prospero's magic, though this is not made clear at this stage.

Once more Prospero robes himself in his cloak and at once changes from a loving father into a mighty magician, and calls Ariel. He is a spirit of the air and is Prospero's servant. We come to know through their dialogue how Ariel had caused the storm and bewildered all the men on board. These men had jumped from the ship and as the island was very near had all swum ashore. None of them suffered any harm. Ariel had been told to divide them into groups and lead them separately to the island. Ferdinand was separated from the rest of them and brought to the island all by himself. The ship itself and the mariners have been safely brought to a harbour and the mariners have been put to sleep. The rest of the fleet which accompanied the king's ship has gone on its way to Naples, thinking that the royal ship has been wrecked and the King, along with all the others, drowned.

Prospero reveals himself as a master planner, with attention to every detail. He had given Ariel all these minute instructions, not forgetting any of the aspects of the matter. Apart from being a mage, he is also a man of organizational abilities.

Prospero praises Ariel for having carried out his instructions so efficiently and then the first reference to time is made. This will happen twice more in the play.

Prospero	:	What is the time o' th' day?
Ariel	:	Past the mid-season.
Prospero	:	At least two glasses. The time 'twixt six and now Must by us be spent most preciously.[6]

It has to be remembered that in this play Shakespeare has observed the classical rules of plot-construction very carefully. This reference to the time points out how carefully he has observed the rule of the unity of time. (For more information on this head see Chapter 9, *infra.*)

Ariel is not happy at the prospect of more work and he starts complaining. Then, through their dialogue we come to know more about the island. Sycorax, a witch, was banished from Algiers to this island. She made Ariel her slave and when he refused to obey her, imprisoned him within a pine tree where he remained confined for twelve years. Meanwhile, Sycorax gave birth to her son Caliban who had the form of a monster. Sycorax, after having imprisoned Ariel, did not have the power to release him and died shortly thereafter. Prospero, when he came to the island, freed Ariel. Yet Ariel is not totally free, he is now the slave of Prospero. Prospero had promised to free him quite soon and now says once more that he will give Ariel his freedom after two days.

The previous history of the island is thus told to the audience and now Prospero tells Ariel to take the shape of an invisible sea-nymph and come to him again. When he does so, Prospero gives him some more instructions.

Prospero then wakes Miranda and summons Caliban. He had tried to educate and civilize Caliban. This had not been entirely successful, for Caliban was not able to take in all this education. He had, however, learnt to speak and also the names of objects. He is vengeful and detests Prospero, whom he regards as an interloper. He thinks that it is he who is the rightful lord of the island and Prospero has wrongfully usurped his place. He had been very friendly towards Prospero at first and Prospero also had been very kind to him, allowing him to sleep in the same cave with himself and Miranda. Caliban, however, was of so gross a nature that he tried to violate Miranda and thereafter Prospero was no longer kind to him and started to treat him like a slave. Miranda too cannot tolerate him and berates him for being ungrateful to her, for she had taught him how to speak and many other things as well. Prospero then sends him to fetch fuel.

The dwellers of the island have now been introduced and their history brought up to date. Shakespeare now turns his attention to other matters. It is time for Ferdinand, the Prince of Naples, to be introduced. He had been present in the foregoing scene, but had not spoken.

Ariel, invisible to him, brings him to Prospero's cave by singing the song "Come unto these yellow sands". As he is invisible to him, Ferdinand follows what he takes to be supernatural music (as in matter of fact it really is).

Ferdinand is under the impression that he is the sole survivor of the ship. Ariel's music soothes his grief at losing his father and he follows it. Now Ariel further allays his grief by singing the famous song. "Full fathom five", speaking of the imperishable quality of nature and of her transforming ability. The mortal earthly human body is changed into a substance of imperishable beauty:

> Of his bones are coral made:
> Those are pearls that were his eyes;
> Nothing of him that doth fade,
> But doth suffer a sea-change
> Into something rich and strange.[7]

Ferdinand has not yet seen Prospero and Miranda but Prospero directs Miranda's attention to him. Miranda, who has never seen any man but her father, thinks him to be a spirit. Prospero tells her that this is a human being and Miranda's reaction convinces him that she is attracted to him:

> I might call him
> A thing divine, for nothing natural
> I ever saw so noble.[8]

Prospero is elated, for this is exactly what he had wanted. Ferdinand, on seeing Miranda, takes her to be the goddess of the island and is overawed by her presence.

Ferdinand introduces himself to Prospero as the King of Naples, for, since he thinks his father to be dead, he himself would now be the king. Ferdinand, on knowing that Miranda is no goddess but a young girl, then and there proposes to her but Prospero will not let things proceed so quickly. He must first prove his love. With this end in view, Prospero begins testing Ferdinand. He accuses Ferdinand of being a spy and orders him to be his (Prospero's) servant. When Ferdinand resists him, Prospero renders him motionless with his magic. Miranda pleads for him and thus evinces her love for him. Prospero then frees Ferdinand and commands him to follow them. Ferdinand's response is that he will deem all griefs as nothing if he can but see Miranda daily.

Elated at the course the events have taken, Prospero gives more instructions to Ariel while Miranda reassures Ferdinand. The long scene then comes to an end, with Prospero still acting as a suspicious and angry father.

This scene, comprising five hundred and two lines, is the longest scene in the play and one of the longest among all the scenes of Shakespeare. It is an expository scene, that is, it acquaints the audience and the reader with all the events that have happened before. It is difficult to impart so much information without being artificial. Shakespeare has solved the problem by making it clear that Miranda is ignorant of all these events. It is but natural that she should be informed at this point, for their lives are about to undergo a drastic change now and she must be prepared for the future.

The dialogue between Prospero and Ariel, on the other hand, is not so natural and unaffected. It is, again, necessary that the audience be informed of the history of the island and this is done by using the question-and-answer method, with Prospero supplying the majority of the answers himself.

Besides acquainting us with Prospero's own history and that of the island, it introduces all the characters on the island and Ferdinand, the romantic hero of the play. Thus the scene is not merely expository but functional as well.

There is another way in which it is even more functional for it shows Ferdinand and Miranda falling in love with each other. Thus one of the themes of the play is introduced. (Please turn to Chapter 6 *infra* for a discussion of the themes of the play.)

The scene is integrally related to the play, for it looks back to the first scene—showing the effects of the storm, and also looks forward to the later scenes. From this point of view it contains a paradoxical element in it, for it contains elements of the past as well as of the future. It is, as a matter of fact, a scene that is unique in itself.

This scene concludes the Act. The first Act thus consists of two scenes—the storm scene, and the expository one. Not much action takes place in this Act, though the first scene is extremely dynamic. The second scene, though it contains the long dialogue between Prospero and Miranda, does not become tedious because of the element of wonder in it, presented by Ariel, who appears once as himself and again as a water-nymph. There are two songs in it as well. Thus the scene has in it two of the elements required in drama—music and spectacle. The main characters have been introduced in this Act and, with the love of Ferdinand and Miranda, the action has started. The Act is functional as well as entertaining.

Act II, Scene i

This scene takes up the royal group of characters. The only such character absent is Ferdinand, and as we last saw him in the foregoing scene, he has been separated from the others. Two more courtiers, Adrian and Francisco, are presented.

Alonso is overwhelmed with grief at the loss of his son who, he thinks, has surely been drowned. Gonzalo tries to comfort him by reminding him of the fact that they themselves are safe. Alonso, in his grief, only wants to be left alone and in peace. Gonzalo persists in trying to comfort him and Antonio and Sebastian, both taking the whole affair very lightly, poke fun at him. We have a very entertaining and witty dialogue, with Gonzalo officiously offering unwanted sympathy and solace and Antonio and Sebastian continually interrupting with light-hearted banter. There is much of word-play in the interjections of these two latter characters. It becomes clear through this dialogue that Alonso, Antonio and Sebastian find nothing pleasant in the island, but, on the other hand, Gonzalo and Adrian find it sweet and friendly:

Adrian	:	It must needs be of subtle, tender and delicate temperance. The air breathes upon us here most sweetly.
Sebastian	:	As if it had lungs, and rotten ones.
Antonio	:	Or as 'twere perfumed by a fen.
Gonzalo	:	Here is everything advantageous to life.
Ant.	:	True, save means to live.
Seb.	:	Of that there's none or little.
Gon.	:	How lush and lusty the grass looks! How green!
Ant.	:	The ground indeed is tawny.
Seb.	:	With an eye of green in't.
Ant.	:	He misses not much.
Seb.	:	No, he doth but mistake the truth to't.[9]

This dialogue is much longer and, beside the grief of Alonso, and the solemnity of Gonzalo, the devil-may-care laughter of Antonio and Sebastian stand as a contrast. What is far more important, as is apparent in the lines quoted above, is the fact that Gonzalo, who is essentially a good and honest man, finds the island pleasant, whereas Antonio and Sebastian, who nourish evil in their heart, find it hostile. It must be remembered that the island is an enchanted one and perhaps Shakespeare seeks to convey the fact that to the good soul it really appears as a beautiful place, but the evil ones really see it as a place hostile to man. The play has deeply philosophical, not to say religious, overtones.

The optimistic outlook of Gonzalo is even more highlighted when he refer to the clothes they are wearing. Their dresses had been drenched in sea-water, yet they appear fresh and shining. These are very fine and expensive clothes that they had worn to attend the marriage of Alonso's daughter at Tunis and they are still as fresh as when first put on. Antonio and Sebastian say that he is telling plain lies. Gonzalo insists on getting an answer from Alonso who finally cries out that he wishes he had never given his daughter in marriage for it is because of that he has now lost his son. They had gone to Tunis in order to attend this wedding so the wedding is indirectly responsible for their present state. He refuses all comforts, though Francisco tells him that maybe Ferdinand has survived the tempest. Sebastian, on the other hand, blames him quite freely for forcing his daughter into a disagreeable marriage.

Then, after having upbraided Sebastian for his utter lack of tact Gonzalo tries to distract everyone by telling them how he would rule the island if he were the lord of it. This is a very important passage and is indebted to the essay *Of the Cannibals* by Montaigne. (Please refer to Chapter 9 *infra* for more details.) He presents the vision of an ideal world where everyone is free and leads on idyllic life in the lap of nature, where nothing is known of the complexities and corruptions of urban life.

Soon after this Ariel enters. He is invisible to all of them and he plays "solemn music". Perhaps it is this music which makes everyone sleep, except Alonso, Antonio and Sebastian. A little later Alonso also falls asleep, whereupon Ariel goes away. Now Antonio starts tempting Sebastian by telling him that he should be the King of Naples. He awakens the ambition dormant in Sebastian's heart and the latter is only too ready to listen to him, and yield to his evil promptings. The King of Naples already has a son and a daughter to inherit his kingdom, but Antonio dismisses them as being of no account, for Ferdinand is definitely dead and Claribel is too far from Naples to be a real threat. He advises Sebastian to kill Alonso and Gonzalo while they are asleep and in return Sebastian promises that he will no longer extract any tribute from him as Alonso had been doing. While they are still talking, however, Ariel arrives and with his song wakens Gonzalo. The others also wake up and Alonso is surprised to see the two plotters with drawn swords in their hands. The two of them escape the wrath of Alonso by making him believe that they had heard the roar of lions.

Ariel had been sent by Prospero who through his magic powers had come to know of the murder-plot. Now Ariel goes off to report to him and the scene ends.

This scene is quite a long one, comprising three hundred and twenty-four lines. It is written both in prose and in verse, for the early part, specially the dialogue with the interjections of Antonio and Sebastian is in prose. Later, with Alonso crying out that he wished he had never married his daughter off at Tunis, verse begins to be spoken. This begins with line no. 101, so nearly a third of the entire scene is in prose. Later again, with Gonzalo losing his patience and administering a mild rebuke to the two callous men, once more prose is spoken for nearly twenty lines. All the characters are noble ones, yet Shakespeare has given prose to them also. This is because the scene, during the comic dialogue, has to be kept on a low level, with the interjections of Antonio and Sebastian producing comic laughter. Later in the part where Antonio persuades Sebastian to consider himself as the rightful king, the scene rises to a serious level and so verse is used. Thus we have a scene which can be clearly divided into two sections, a light one and a serious one, with Gonzalo's speech on the commonwealth serving as a turning-point and Ariel's music serving as the dividing line. Then, from line two hundred onwards the murder-plot comes into prominence. This part is entirely in verse. The poet has used the Elizabethan convention of using a mixture of prose and verse to highlight the different sections of the scene. There is music of the vocal as well as the instrumental kind. The instrumental music puts the characters to sleep and Ariel's song wakes Gonzalo up.

The scene introduces both evil and good to us. Gonzalo the good character sees the island as a pleasant place, a fit place for the ideal commonwealth. Antonio and Sebastian see it as barren and hostile because there is a core of evil in both of them that has twisted their outlook. Alonso, though he had helped Antonio to overthrow his brother, is shown as suffering the grief of losing his son, and it is known that suffering purifies the human soul. He is, therefore, on the way to deserving Prospero's forgiveness.

Act II, scene ii

This, as opposed to the former scene, is entirely comic in character. Here we see the humbler characters of the ship and their encounter with Caliban. It is Caliban who opens the scene with a curse for Prospero. He recounts how Prospero often punished him by making spirits take the forms of many different animals and tease him. When he sees Trinculo come, Caliban supposes him to be a spirit sent by Prospero and tries to hide from him.

Trinculo is a jester. Looking down he sees Caliban lying covered with a cloak. Caliban, it has to be remembered, is a monster. He has a humanoid shape, but is different from humans. To Trinculo he looks rather like a creature between a man and a fish. He sees that it is a living creature. Meanwhile a storm is coming on and, as there is no shelter nearby, Trinculo creeps under Caliban's cloak.

Stephano now enters. He too is a comic character—a drunken butler. He enters already drunk and continues drinking and singing. His attention wanders to Caliban when the latter cries out. Since Trinculo is also hiding under the cloak, Stephano looks down and sees four legs, not two. He thinks that here is a wild animal who is sick, and offers him drink to cure his ague. Now Trinculo, recognising Stephano's voice, thinks that since Stephano has got drowned, this is a devil.

Stephano, on the other hand, hearing two voices, thinks that here is an animal with two voices:

> Four legs and two voices; a most delicate monster.
> ...If all the wine in my bottle will recover him, I
> will help his ague.[10]

Stephano and Trinculo then discover each other. While they are talking Caliban, having tasted wine for the first time, decides that it is no earthly drink and Stephano is a god. He assumes that Stephano has come from the heavens above and Stephano, amused, says that he is the man from the moon. Caliban, fully convinced, swears allegiance to him. He is prepared to work for Stephano and take him to the best places in the island. So the three of them set out, with Caliban singing a drunken song, which is the fifth song in the play.

This is a comic scene, and serves as a foil to the serious scene preceding it. This, too, is written in a mixture of prose and verse. It has to be noted that Shakespeare has given poetry to Caliban though he is a monster, and prose to Stephano and Trinculo though they are human beings. In addition to providing laughter, the scene also contains two songs. Both of them are drinking songs, the first sung by Stephano and the second by Caliban. It also gives, through Trinculo, a description of Caliban which is the only such description in the entire play.

This scene ends the Act. Like the first Act, this also contains only two scenes. The first scene contains a long comic dialogue, but after that, with the murder-plot, the scene presents evil in a serious form. The second scene, with its innocent comedy, is a contrast to it. This is another feature of Shakespeare's dramaturgy, that he arranges his scenes as contrasts to one another. In Act I also we have the storm-scene which is extremely dynamic and serious, contrasting with the calm serenity of the next scene. Here also, the same feature is to be noted. The scene introduces us to the comic characters—Trinculo and Stephano who at present are purely comic ones, with no evil in them. A careless good nature is also present in them, for they take Caliban in tow, though it might be out of selfishness. They are strangers to the island and Caliban offers them worshipful adoration, as well as the promise of allaying their hunger. But this comes later. It must be remembered to Stephano's credit that, thinking Caliban to be a sick animal, he tries to cure him by offering the little that he has—a bottle of sack. This argues a kind and helpful nature.

Act III, scene i

This is the famous log-bearing scene in which Ferdinand and Miranda declare their love for each other. Ferdinand is patiently carrying out Prospero's orders who had told him to take logs of wood to his cell. Ferdinand is a prince and this kind of work is below his dignity, yet he does it willingly, for he has fallen in love with Miranda.

While he is carrying a log Miranda enters. Unknown to her, Prospero has accompanied her invisibly. He remains invisible to both of them while the audience can see him and hear his comments. We thus have a situation fraught with dramatic irony. Miranda has been forbidden to speak to Ferdinand, so, in coming to meet him, she is disobeying Prospero. The overwhelming force of her love is presented by Shakespeare through these two characters by making both of them break their lifelong habits.

Miranda is full of sympathy for Ferdinand and tells him to rest while she herself will carry the logs which Ferdinand firmly refuses to do. He asks her name and she tells him, becoming instantly conscious that she has disobeyed her father in doing so. Ferdinand tells her that he has seen many ladies, but none like her:

> But you, O you,
> So perfect and so peerless, are created
> Of every creature's best.[11]

Miranda is equally frank. She has been brought up in the lap of nature; no one has taught her to be coy or flirtatious. She does exactly as her heart tells her to do:

> I would not wish
> Any companion in the world but you,
> Nor can imagination form a shape
> Besides yourself to like of.[12]

She frankly asks him whether he loves her or not and when he swears that he does, she weeps because she feels unworthy of him. They solemnly promise to love each other and marry.

Prospero, totally invisible, oversees the entire scene and is elated. This is exactly what he had wanted:

> Fair encounter
> Of two most rare affections! Heavens rain grace
> On that which breeds between them![13]

This is a short but very important scene, for it was to this end that Prospero had directed all his plans.

Act III, scene ii

This is again a scene which, like the second scene of the first Act, is both serious and comic in tone. This scene concerns itself with the comic characters, Stephano and Trinculo along with Caliban. After some comic dialogue, Caliban tells Stephano about Prospero, presenting him as a usurper. He tells Stephano that he himself will become the lord of the island if he kills Prospero and then Caliban will serve him faithfully. So here, as in Act I sc. ii, another murder-plot is hatched. While Caliban is telling all this Ariel, invisible, overhears the plot.

Stephano and Trinculo agree, then they all sing a song the tune to which is played by Ariel. As Ariel is invisible the two of them are afraid of this music and Caliban, in a famous speech, reassures them:

> Be not afeard, the isle is full of noises,
> Sounds and sweet airs, that give delight and hurt not.[14]

The scene is quite brief, containing only a hundred and fifty lines. Shakespeare uses both prose and verse in it. The two comic characters speak in prose but Caliban in verse. It contains both instrumental and vocal music. What is far more remarkable is the manner in which Shakespeare has mingled comic and serious effects in the scene. From this point of view as well as others it can be compared with the second scene of Act I. There also the two characters Antonio and Sebastian continue poking fun at Gonzalo and then the second part of the scene shows the presence of evil through the murder-plot. In this scene also there is simultaneous presence of comic and serious effects. It is only when Caliban unfolds the plot to kill Prospero that evil intrudes. Ariel's interjections ("Thou liest" three times) provide a comic parallel to the former scene.

Act III, scene iii

This scene takes up the royal party. Everyone is tired and depressed. Gonzalo cannot walk any further and Alonso is now giving up hopes of finding his son. The two conspirators are still intent on their evil scheme. They have been foiled once, but they will seize the next opportunity. In fact they decide to kill Alonso that very night.

At this point Prospero appears aloft. The Elizabethan stage had a gallery or balcony at the back of the stage, and Prospero appears there. He is invisible to the characters on the stage. Now a strange spectacle is presented.

Solemn music is heard and strange beings bring in a feast for the characters. They are surprised and Gonzalo points out that these creatures are better-mannered than many at Naples.

As soon as they prepare to eat the food thus provided, Ariel appears in the form of a harpy. These are monsters from Greek myths, being creatures shaped like birds but with the faces of women. As soon as Ariel appears the food vanishes and then Ariel delivers a diatribe terrible enough to frighten anyone. He tells them that they are men of sin and Destiny has cast them on this uninhabited island because they are not fit to live among men. When the others draw their swords he tells them that he and other creatures like him are the agents of Fate and nothing can harm them. It is a long speech and he goes on to tell them that because they had left Prospero and Miranda to perish in the sea, the sea is now taking revenge and has cast them upon this island where they will suffer a lingering death. He then vanishes to the sound of thunder, leaving consternation behind him.

Prospero's pleasure at the effective way in which Ariel has carried out his orders is intense and now he goes off to have a look at Ferdinand. Alonso then speaks in moving words, signifying how his conscience has awakened and he is overcome with remorse. He is convinced that it is because of this sin of his that Ferdinand has been taken from him. Antonio and Sebastian, however, remain unmoved.

This scene, more than any other, has the element of wonder in it. Not only does Ariel appear as a harpy but other strange creatures also. The spreading of the feast and its vanishing is no less a matter for wonder. The scene accomplishes one important purpose—the awakening of Alonso's conscience to remorse. The other two, however, are not so easily affected. Alonso has lost his son and grief has made his heart softer but neither Antonio nor Sebastian has had any such purifying experience. Be that as it may, Prospero's purposes are being gradually fulfilled, as he expected.

The scene is entirely in verse, and quite serious in tone. The presence of evil is highlighted but the way to repentance and forgiveness is also kept open. Alonso's repentance is expressed in one of Shakespeare's most moving passages:

> O, it is monstrous, monstrous!
> Methought the billows spoke and told me of it,
> The winds did sing it to me; and the thunder,
> That deep and dreadful organ-pipe, pronounced
> The name of Prospero: it did bass my trespass.[15]

The scene is highly relevant to the action and is linked with earlier as well as later scenes. Alonso had not given up the hope of finding his son and so all of them had been looking for Ferdinand in the place where we saw them last. This scene begins with a reference to this search and thus can be taken as a continuation of the former scene (Act II, sc. i). It looks forward to the later scenes as well for Gonzalo directs the other courtiers to keep watch on the three culprits and they all leave the stage following Alonso, Antonio and Sebastian.

This scene brings Act III to an end. It has been a very eventful Act, continuing as it does, with the love-affair of Ferdinand and Miranda in the log-bearing scene, the murder-plot is begun and the characters, particularly Alonso, are led towards repentance. All the three scenes of this Act are highly functional and take the action forward. It contains the element of music as well as of spectacle—two requirements of drama as given by Aristotle. The element of wonder is present throughout the play, but in this scene this feature has been highlighted by the banquet scene. All in all it is an effective and eventful Act.

Act IV, scene i

Shakespeare brings us back to the main characters once more. Prospero is in a benign mood. He assures Ferdinand that all the humiliations to which he had been subjected had been inflicted on him to test the sincerity of his love. Now all the trials are over and Prospero gives Miranda to him as his bride:

> All thy vexations
> Were but trials of thy love, and thou
> Hast strangely stood the test. Here, afore heaven,
> I ratify this my rich gift.[16]

Prospero then warns Ferdinand that this is a betrothal and not a marriage. He, therefore, must not take any unseemly liberties with Miranda. She is innocent and pure and must remain so, till the marriage ceremony has taken place. Ferdinand assures him of his compliance. This warning is delivered once more a few lines later.

Prospero, both to entertain them and to celebrate the betrothal, then calls Ariel and tells him to call the other spirits over whom Ariel rules. Then a masque is presented in which spirits enact the roles of goddesses.

The goddess Iris, the rainbow-goddess who is also the messenger of the gods, appears. Calling on Ceres, she tells her that Juno has called her. Then Juno's chariot appears, but does not yet descend to the stage. Ariel acts as Ceres.

Iris tells Ceres that she has been called to celebrate and bless the union of two true lovers. Ceres agrees and then Juno's chariot descends on the stage and Juno calls Ceres to join her. Once more the chariot rises with the two goddesses and both of them sing a song of blessing. Nymphs and peasants are then called in and they dance a joyful dance.

Suddenly Prospero remembers the murder-plot against him. He is extremely annoyed and tells the spirits to leave.

Now, in a famous speech he tells Ferdinand and Miranda how everything, like the masque they have just seen, is transitory. The actors in the masque were invisible airy spirits and as soon as the masque was over, they vanished into air. Drawing an analogy between the masque and the real world, he points out that one is as evanescent as the other:

> These our actors,
> As I foretold you, were all spirits, and
> Are melted into air, into thin air,
> And, like the baseless fabrics of this vision
> The cloud-capp'd towers, the gorgeous palaces
> The solemn temples, the great globe itself,
> Yea, all which it doth inherit, shall dissolve,
> And like this insubstantial pageant faded
> Leave not a wrack behind. We are such stuff
> As dreams are made on, and our little life
> Is rounded with a sleep.[17]

He then excuses himself and sends the lovers off to get some rest. There is no rest, however, for him. Now he calls Ariel and asks him what he has done with the three plotters. Ariel tells him that he has led them to a pool of filthy water where they still are. Prospero praises Ariel and then sends him to bring some worthless finery to attract these low-class clowns. Ariel brings shining clothes and hangs them on the trees nearby.

While Prospero and Ariel remain invisible, the three plotters enter and seeing the fine clothes, put them on, though they themselves are covered with mud. Prospero then conjures up a whole group of spirits shaped like dogs and hounds, and sets them after the three of them.

The scene ends here. It is a long scene and makes up an entire Act. Naturally, therefore, there are many different events that take place in it: the young lovers are blessed and formally betrothed to each other, the masque is presented and the comic characters are discomfited.

Once again we find serious and comic actions juxtaposed in the same scene. As has been seen in the earlier scenes also, Shakespeare, in this play, often mingles serious and comic events in the same scene. So the first part of the scene is serious, then, with the entrance of Stephano, Trinculo and Caliban, the comic element predominates.

The scene is written in a mixture of verse and prose. The first part is in verse, and prose is introduced with the entrance of the comic characters. Here also it has to be noted that though Stephano and Trinculo speak in prose, Caliban does not. There are also passages in couplets. Prior to this we have seen the use of single couplets at the end of scenes, but here in the masque couplets have been used in the dialogues between Iris and Ceres—a dialogue of more than forty lines. In addition there are songs in the scene. There is a short song of only five lines by Ariel and then there is a duet sung by Juno and Ceres to bless the young couple and sanctify the betrothal.

The scene, though long, never becomes tedious as there is plenty of variety in it. It brings one part of Prospero's plans (the marriage of Ferdinand and Miranda) to fulfilment and punishes the three comic plotters. Thus the scene is integrally related to the play. Moreover, it brings together the characters of the main plot and the sub-plot, for the first time. There is no interaction between the two groups, for Prospero and Ariel remain invisible, but at least Prospero punishes them.

Act V, scene i

The play is drawing to a close and this is the only scene in this, the last, Act. First of all it presents Prospero in his magic robes. He had appeared in them in the second scene of Act I and now he has donned them once more.

Shakespeare calls attention to the time for the third time in the play. Prospero asks Ariel what the time is and Ariel says it is the sixth hour. Prospero had said in the second scene of the first Act that he will have to finish his work by this time and Ariel reminds him of this. Prospero then asks him about the condition of the royal party. Ariel gives a truly moving description of how they are desperately penitent, driven almost mad by the consciousness of their guilt. He ends by pleading in favour of them:

> Your charm so strongly works them
> That if you now beheld them, your affections
> Would become tender.[18]

Prospero is moved and resolves to have pity on the miscreants:

> The rarer action is
> In virtue than in vengeance. They being penitent
> The sole drift of my purpose doth extend
> Not a frown further.[19]

He sends Ariel off to fetch them and when Ariel has gone he does something extremely significant. First of all he draws a magic circle on the stage and then addresses all the spirits of the island who are under his command. He describes how, with their help, he had performed many awe-inspiring feats:

> I have bedimm'd
> The noontide sun, call'd forth the mutinous winds,
> And 'twixt the green sea and the azur'd vault
> Set roaring war.[20]

He has, however, reached such a high state of maturity that he now calls these powers "rough magic" and renounces them.

> But this rough magic
> I hereby abjure . . . .
> . . . . I'll break my staff
> Bury it certain fathoms in the earth
> And deeper than did ever plummet sound
> I'll drown my book.[21]

This long speech describes Prospero's power over the forces of nature as well as supernatural spirits. All this is renounced in a gesture that has hardly been paralleled by any other dramatic character. The serious student will do well to read J.M. Barrie's play *The Admirable Crichton* in which the same action is repeated by the hero.

At this point in the play Prospero rises to a height of nobility which makes it clear that his past sufferings have purged his character of all its impurities. He has conquered greed for power so that he is able to renounce it, and he has also conquered his desire for revenge. It is a paradoxical fact that by giving up his powers he becomes far more majestic and awesome than he had been before.

Now Ariel comes in followed by the royal characters. They enter the charmed circle Prospero had drawn, and are still under his spell. Prospero has some music played and gradually the charm wears off. While this is happening Prospero addresses each of the culprits in a long speech, expressing his gratitude to Gonzalo and forgiving each of his enemies. He realises that none of them will recognise him in his present form. So he dresses himself like a nobleman by putting on his hat and rapier and directs Ariel to go to the ship and bring the captain and the Boatswain to this place.

The others recover their senses. Prospero addresses Alonso first and embraces him to prove that he himself is a living being and no ghost. Alonso is convinced:

> Since I saw thee
> Th' affliction of my mind amends, with which
> I fear a madness held me....
> Thy dukedom I resign and do entreat
> Thou pardon me my wrongs.[22]

Prospero then embraces Gonzalo and then turns to Sebastian and Antonio. He tells both of them that he knows about their plot against Alonso, but he is not going to say anything about it at present. Perhaps this is because he knows that the element of evil is so strong in them that they cannot be reformed, so he keeps this knowledge as a weapon. He is stern with them and though he forgives Antonio, leaves him in no doubt about his opinion of his character. He also asks Antonio formally to return his duchy to him.

Alonso then tells Prospero that he has lost his son and Prospero tells him that he has lost a daughter. This, of course, is figuratively true, as the audience understands, but not the King of Naples. Instead he exclaims:

> A daughter?
> O heavens, that they were living both in Naples
> The king and queen there![23]

This does but fulfil Prospero's heart's desires. Now he tells Alonso that as he has restored his dukedom to him, he will in turn give him something as good. Saying this, he draws a curtain and reveals Ferdinand and Miranda sitting, playing chess. As soon as Ferdinand becomes aware of their presence, he comes and kneels to his father, asking for his blessing. Both are naturally overjoyed to see each other. It is now that Miranda says those rapturous lines:

O wonder!
How many goodly creatures are there here!
How beauteous mankind is! O brave new world
That hath such people in it![24]

It is Gonzalo to whom Shakespeare gives the lines that sum up the joyful occasion with blessings:

Was Milan thrust from Milan that his issue
Should become kings of Naples? O rejoice
Beyond a common joy and set it down
With gold on lasting pillars.[25]

Now Ariel brings in the Master of the ship and the Boatswain. The latter assures them that the ship is safe and as good as new. Everyone is puzzled and Prospero tells them that everything will be explained to them at a convenient time. Then he sends Ariel off to bring the comic characters. Caliban, on seeing Prospero with the other characters, realises how fine and noble they all are, specially in comparison with Stephano and Trinculo. The others cannot recognise them, so Prospero introduces Caliban to them and tells them of the plot they had hatched to kill him. Alonso recognises his butler and his jester. Prospero directs Caliban to prepare his cell for receiving the royal guests and Caliban, his eyes opened now, responds with willing obedience:

I'll be wise hereafter
And seek for grace. What a thrice-double ass
Was I to take this drunk for a god,
And worship this dull fool![26]

Prospero now invites everyone to his cell. He tells Ariel that the last work he will have to do will be to convey their ship safely to Naples and thereafter he shall be totally free.

This is a long scene and makes up the entire fifth Act by itself. There are many plays of Shakespeare in which the last Act comprises only one scene, and this is one of them. It is the denouement of the play and brings the action to a conclusion. It is mainly in verse but there are a few lines of prose as well, spoken by the comic characters. It also contains the song that Ariel sings in joyful anticipation of his freedom.

It is a scene that highlights the motif of fulfilment. Everyone gets his heart's desire. Prospero gets his dukedom and a son-in-law, Alonso gets his son and a daughter-in-law, Ariel gets his freedom. It has not been pointed out in the play, but after the entire party leaves the island, Caliban will be left in possession of the island which is exactly what he had wanted.

Prospero, however, has to give up more than he gets, for he has to renounce his magic powers and has to forgive his enemies. Both of these are done willingly. He had given up all thoughts of revenge quite early in the play and freely forgives his enemies. As a matter of fact he is a character who gives far more than he gets.

The Epilogue

The Tempest is one of the few plays of Shakespeare which has an Epilogue designated as such. It is spoken by Prospero. He now comes forward and addresses the audience in his own character and not as an actor who has completed his work in the play. Instead he tells the audience that it is only by their gracious permission that he can go back to his own cell. It is as if the audience had cast a spell on him and confined him to the island. Now he requests them to break the spell by clapping their hands so that he can be set free.

This Epilogue is written in couplets and not in blank verse like the poetry used in the rest of the play. It brings the play to a neat end, yet looks forward to the future. It emphasizes the moral vision of the play:

> And my ending is despair
> Unless I be relieved by prayer.
> Which pierces so that it assaults
> Mercy itself and frees all faults.

As you from crimes would pardon'd be
Let your indulgence set me free.

Thus Prospero, as is but fitting, has the last words in the play.

REFERENCES

1. Act I, sc. i, lines 13-14, p. 1.
2. Act I, sc. i, *ll.* 65-66, p. 3.
3. Act I, sc. i, *ll.* 19-23, p. 2.
4. Act I, sc. ii, *ll.* 1-2, p. 4.
5. Act I, sc. ii, *ll.* 75-77, p. 7.
6. Act I, sc. ii, *ll.* 239-41, p. 14.
7. Act I, sc. ii, *ll.* 398-402, p. 21.
8. Act I, sc. ii, *ll.* 418-20, p. 21.
9. Act II, sc. i, *ll.* 42-56, p. 29.
10. Act II, sc. ii, *ll.* 88-92, p. 43.
11. Act III, sc. i, *ll.* 46-48, p. 50.
12. Act III, sc. i, *ll.* 54-57, p. 50.
13. Act III, sc. i, *ll.* 74-76, p. 51.
14. Act III, sc. ii, *ll.* 133-34, p. 57.
15. Act III, sc. iii, *ll.* 95-99, p. 62.
16. Act IV, sc. i, *ll.* 5-8, p. 63.
17. Act IV, sc. i, *ll.* 148-58, p. 70.
18. Act V, sc. i, *ll.* 17-19, p. 76.
19. Act V, sc. i, *ll.* 27-30, p. 76.
20. Act V, sc. i, *ll.* 41-44, p. 77.
21. Act V, sc. i, *ll.* 50-57, p. 77.
22. Act V, sc. i, *ll.* 115-19, p. 79.
23. Act V, sc. i, *ll.* 149-50, p. 81.
24. Act V, sc. i, *ll.* 181-84, p. 82.
25. Act V, sc. i, *ll.* 294-97, p. 86.
26. Act V, sc. i, *ll.* 333-38, p. 88.

6

The Major Themes

There are many elements that function as the unifying factor of a play and its theme is one of them. In certain cases, as with *The Tempest*, the theme is not merely one of the unifying factors but, as a matter of fact, overshadows the other elements like the plot, etc. in importance. In the last romances Shakespeare has embodied his mature vision of the world and of life. Even though the play is like a fairytale, the moral vision overrides the romance and the enchantment. When one takes up a play which deals, like *The Tempest*, with the same element of the romance and the fairytale, the difference becomes quite obvious. *A Midsummer Night's Dream* also deals with young lovers and enchantment, and these become the pre-dominating elements. In *The Tempest* everything else is swept aside when one comes to the theme. There are, in fact, several themes in the play.

(a) The Theme of Freedom

This is one of the dominant themes of the play and can be understood in a superficial way as well as at a deeper level. At the superficial level there is the thirst for freedom evinced primarily by Ariel and in a lesser degree by Caliban. The concept is produced in the second scene:

Prospero : What is it thou canst demand?
Ariel : My Liberty.[1]

Prospero has already set him free from a truly terrible imprisonment, yet he is still a slave. He wants to be totally free. Throughout the play there are recurring references to the freedom he looks forward to, both by Prospero and by himself, rising to a climax in the wonderful song in which he anticipates his freedom in the last Act: "Where the bee sucks, there suck I."

A much more serious interpretation of the theme of freedom has been given by the Victorian critic Edward Dowden:

> A thought which seems to run through the whole of *The Tempest*, appearing here and there like a coloured thread in some web, is the thought that the true freedom of man consists in servitude.[2]

The characters, each in his own way, discover this truth. Ferdinand finds that service, undertaken willingly, will bring him closer to Miranda:

> This my mean task
> Would be as heavy to me, as odious, but
> The mistress which I serve quickens what's dead
> And makes my labours pleasant.[3]

He gains freedom not only from this temporary slavery but also gains Miranda by serving Prospero in a willing and obedient manner. He sees himself as in glorious servitude to Miranda:

> The very instant that I saw you, did
> My heart fly to your service, there resides
> To make me slave to it.[4]

Miranda also is not only ready to share his present servitude but also to serve him throughout her life:

> I am your wife if you will marry me;
> If not, I'll die your maid.[5]

Their willingness to undergo service is rewarded by giving them more than their hearts' desire. Ferdinand not only gets Miranda but his father also and Miranda becomes, besides the wife of Ferdinand, the future queen of Naples, with the joyous approval of her father-in-law, Alonso.

Prospero also talks of freedom in the Epilogue. It is as if he has been exiled to the island by the magic of the audience and he now begs to be freed:

Now 'tis true
I must be here confined by you
Or sent to Naples. Let me not
Since I have my dukedom got,
And pardon'd the deceiver, dwell
In this bare island by your spell
But release me from my bands.[6]

Another instance of the importance given to the concept of freedom is to be found in Gonzalo's description of an imaginary commonwealth. This is to be a society totally free from all servitude or force.

...no name of magistrate;
Letters should not be known, riches, poverty,
And use of service, none contract, succession,
Bourn, bound of land, tilth, vinyard, none;[7]

There is to be total freedom in this utopia imagined by him. It is his concept of the Golden Age, and the concept of freedom is extended even to nature. Gonzalo says that there should be no use of force in any way. Even nature should produce without any force:

All things in common nature should produce
Without sweat or endeavour . . . .
. . . . nature should bring forth
Of its own kind all foison, all abundance
To feed my innocent people.[8]

There are thus three kinds of freedom present in the play: freedom *from* servitude as represented by Ariel, freedom *in* servitude as given out in the cases of Ferdinand and Miranda, and total freedom as is conceived by Gonzalo for his utopia.

(b) Obliteration of Evil through Love

This is definitely one of the major themes of the play—not only of this play but of all the last romances. In all of them the same theme, with some variations, is illustrated. Moreover, this theme involves two generations, for one generation propagates evil and the next generation obliterates it. J. Middleton Murry has called attention to this feature.

> It may be that his central idea was the obliteration of the evil done and suffered by one generation through the love of the next.[9]

The story as told by Shakespeare justifies this claim. Prospero, when telling Miranda of their early history, emphasizes the evil he had suffered again and again. Both Alonso and Antonio were culprits. Not only did Antonio betray his trustful brother, he also betrayed his own country. He became the Duke of Milan by deposing his brother, which is high treason, by planning to kill him and his innocent daughter and finally by selling the freedom of his country. He is thus guilty of: high treason, of intended murder, and of betraying his country. Alonso conspired with him; therefore he too is guilty though his guilt is not as serious as that of Antonio. Prospero himself is not guiltless either, and he freely confesses this:

> those being all my study,
> The government I cast upon my brother,
> And to my state grew stranger, being transported
> And rapt in secret studies.[10]

Later he expresses himself in clearer and more emphatic language, taking the blame not only of neglecting his duties but of tempting his brother:

> I thus neglecting worldly ends, all dedicated
> To closeness and the bettering of my mind
> With that which, but by being so retir'd,
> O'er-priz'd all popular rate, in my false brother
> Awak'd an evil nature.[11]

He thus takes the moral responsibility for the heinous action of his brother. Thus feeling indirectly guilty, it is not surprising that he should think of forgiving his enemies, which he does willingly.

The younger generation is represented by Ferdinand and Miranda. In all the four plays of this group the younger generation is depicted as pure and innocent. The love they feel for each other is equally pure, without a trace of selfishness or egotism. It is a love that is fully capable of washing away the sins of the parents. Ferdinand's father had been an inveterate enemy of Prospero, had overthrown him and had not prevented Antonio from setting them adrift in a manner that could only bring death. Now his son is prepared to serve Prospero and would deem it a reward if he does but get a glimpse of Miranda every day. It is a pure, noble, chivalrous love that he offers to Miranda.

Miranda too does not lag behind. Prospero is mindful and repentant of his neglect of his administrative duties, but he does not neglect his duties as a single parent. He has brought her up single-handed, being her father, mother and teacher, all in one. He has made Miranda a frank and honest girl full of all womanly virtues like modesty and obedience, pity, etc. Her love is so strong that she disobeys her father for the first time and comes to Ferdinand in secret. There is never any doubt of the strong and enduring quality of the love of these two young lovers. Whatever mistakes the earlier generation had made, whatever injuries they had inflicted on each other through egotism and greed are thus washed away by the purity and selfless love of the young people.

(c) The Theme of Regeneration

This, like the theme mentioned above, is a theme common to all the Last Romances and is indirectly related to the theme of the obliteration of evil by a younger generation. In each of the Last Romances we find two generations and the older generation, by the end of the play, is replaced by a purer and younger generation. This theme is essentially an idealistic one, for Shakespeare in his later years finds that the older a man grows, the more worldly-wise does he become and this involves loss of purity and innocence. He shows, for example, a man bringing death and destruction to his own family by his own vicious nature as in King Leontes in *The Winter's Tale*. At the end of the play this corrupt and intemperate generation withdraws and life is carried on by a purer younger generation, for example Florizel and Perdita in this play.

In *The Tempest* he repeats the same theme. The corrupt and ambitious brother of Prospero is punished. Prospero himself, through twelve long years of self-analysis and repentance, changes out of his former negligence, withdrawn self into a far better person. Ferdinand and Miranda (who is the very embodiment of purity and innocence) step in to make the world a better place. E.M.W. Tillyard points out:

> Not only do Ferdinand and Miranda sustain Prospero in representing a new order of things that has evolved out of destruction; they also vouch for its continuation.[12]

In a way *The Tempest* is different from the other plays of this group in that Prospero is a far more positive character than Pericles, Cymbeline or Leontes. He is guilty only of neglecting his duty which is not a very serious crime. Moreover, he is severely punished for this one shortcoming in his character. He is not only deposed but sent out of his own country and made to face a terrible lingering death not only of himself but of his only child. Then, "by divine providence," he reaches the island where, through twelve long years he, suffering and learning, evolves into a wise and truly noble person. This play thus shows regeneration, not only through a younger generation, but regeneration in Prospero himself. It is not that he does not retire from worldly life. He renounces his magic powers, but he accepts the duties of dukedom. He does this in a spirit of humility:

> And thence retire me to my Milan, where
> Every third thought should be my grave.[13]

In the Epilogue also Shakespeare stresses this attitude of spiritual maturity:

> And my ending is despair
> Unless I be reliev'd by prayer,
> Which pierces so that it assaults
> Mercy itself and frees all faults.[14]

This Prospero is very different from the Prospero of twelve years ago who had been thrown out by his treacherous brother. There has been a complete regeneration of his own character. A better, more Christian Prospero is now holding the centre of the stage, a Prospero who attained an awesome nobility when he renounced his magical powers. The theme of regeneration, therefore, gives us not just a purer younger generation, but a new and nobler Prospero as well. This new Prospero is one who has realised the importance of working among and through other human beings in ordinary society. His power in the island had been absolute, but over non-human creatures. Now he has to go back to his dukedom and mingle with ordinary men:

> His wisdom makes him return to his rightful place as a governor of himself and, as a governor, through his dukedom, of other human beings as well.[15]

The theme of regeneration, moreover, assumes great importance because it is a part of life and of Nature. The seasonal cycle presents us with continual renewal in nature. Every year with the coming of winter the old world dies and in spring new life is created. The cycle of death and rebirth is thus as old as Nature herself, and this gives a special dimension to this particular theme.

(d) The Theme of Natural Life

It is Frank Kermode's opinion that in *The Tempest* Shakespeare has taken up the theme of Nature and the influence of Man (or Art) on her. This is a common theme in Elizabethan literature. Man is shown in his relationship with nature and this is looked upon from mainly two points of view. There is, on one hand, the vision of nature as pure, innocent and benevolent. Man introduces corruption into this ideal pastoral world. On the other hand there is the picture of a nature in which there is much that is wild and barbarous and would benefit by man's careful art. Shakespeare presents both the views in an analytical and sympathetic manner. Nature, to him, is a complex entity, not to be fitted up with a label in a simplistic manner:

> Shakespeare's treatment of the theme has what all his mature poetry has, a richly analytical approach to ideas, which never reaches after a naked opinion of true or false.[16]

Thus the play gives an uninhabited island which is not a hostile one, though it is not inhabited by man. Nature has poured forth her treasures in it. Adrian finds the air sweet and

Gonzalo finds everything in it that man may need to live simply and peacefully. He indeed finds it to be an ideal place for founding the ideal utopia. The island holds forth the possibilities of a golden age to him. It is like the primal Garden of Eden to him, where corruption has not entered yet. We come to know too, from Caliban, that there are pleasant and fertile spots in the island. He had shown them to Prospero and Miranda when they had come to the island, and he is ready to show them to Stephano and Trinculo as he accepts them as gods from the moon.

This is the positive, ideal and pastoral aspect of nature. Yet Shakespeare does not fail to point out the negative aspects through the character of Caliban who represents nature:

> Prospero is, therefore, the representative of Art, as Caliban is of Nature.[17]

Caliban is savage and wild. There is much in him that needs to be corrected. Yet Prospero, though he could teach Caliban how to talk, had not been able to really civilize him. No amount of effort on Prospero's part to nurture him has been successful:

> A devil, a born devil, on whose nature
> Nurture can never stick, on whom my pains
> Humanely taken, all, all lost, quite lost.[18]

Caliban, thus, represents that aspect of Nature which is wild and has to be tamed, which is barbarous and has to be civilized. Prospero's Art was not able to triumph over this unruly and savage aspect of Nature. In the last analysis, the island is left behind with Caliban as its sole lord. Gonzalo's commonwealth has not been established, nor has Caliban been civilized. It is not clear whether Nature triumphs over Art or *vice versa*. Shakespeare leaves it open.

(e) The Theme of Order and Chaos

This concept of the central theme of the play echoes the ideas discussed above in a slightly different manner. Prospero is now seen as an exercise of order over the forces of chaos:

> Prospero, of course, is the centre of order, but Ferdinand and Miranda, under his tutelage, become agents of order.[19]

There are thus the forces of order and the forces of chaos in the play. The best example of the latter is Caliban, whose wildness defies all attempts of Prospero to civilize him. Prospero, like an artist, tries to impose order on chaos. He exercises control over the island by his magic power and by music. All impulses of rebellion are quelled by his magic (for example he induces a state of stillness in Ferdinand when the latter wants to defy him). Murder-plots, which are the means by which chaos can come, are foiled by his foreknowledge and alertness. When disorder threatens the other characters after the harpy-scene, he puts them in a state of trance. This last condition has been repeatedly highlighted in the play. Describing the three culprits Ariel says:

> The king
> His brother, and yours, abide all three distracted.[20]

Gonzalo, on being released from the spell, says:

> All torments, trouble, wonder and amazement
> Inhabit here.[21]

Alonso, on being embraced by Prospero, can hardly believe his eyes. He had been deeply disturbed and he feels far more balanced now:

> Since I saw thee
> Th'affliction of my mind amends, with what
> I fear a madness, held me.[22]

Prospero, thus, exercises benevolent control over all of them, restoring order and sanity to their minds. His is the power that brings order out of chaos—a positive, benign magic.

Yet there is one over whom his power fails. Just as Frank Kermode sees Caliban representing nature, so Rose Zimbardo sees him as the representative of chaos: "Caliban, the incarnation of chaos." Just as Prospero is the centre of the force of order, so Caliban is the centre of the forces of disorder:

> If Gonzalo, Ferdinand and Miranda with Prospero to the fore are the creators of and submitters to a system of order, Antonio, Sebastian, Stephano and Trinculo with Caliban in the centre are creators of disorder.[23]

In this conflict between order and chaos, Prospero imposes order and system on everyone excepting Caliban. Though Prospero thinks that all his efforts to educate him have been in vain, Shakespeare gives us an indication that his eyes have been opened, he is no longer rebellious and is a willing servant at the end. He replies to Prospero's order to prepare his cell for the guests:

> Ay, that I will; and I'll be wise hereafter
> And seek for grace. What a thrice double ass
> Was I to take this drunk for a god.[24]

He is left in possession of the island, but to the end Prospero thinks that he remains unregenerate and dismisses him as one unworthy of further attempts. This is being unfair to Caliban. He had learnt how to speak, which is greatly to his credit. Moreover, constant association with beings superior to himself had refined him to some extent. When Stephano and Trinculo sing the wrong tune, he points it out, though the men remain unaware.

(f) The Theme of Struggle for Power and Usurpation

This is a dominant theme in the play, and everyone indulges in it. All the characters except Ferdinand and Miranda are struggling for power, dethroning others and usurping their place. Jan Kott has expatiated on this theme:

> Prospero's narration is a description of a struggle for power...the same theme will be repeated in the story of Ariel and Caliban.[25]

Their previous history, as told by Prospero to Miranda, shows the lust for power in Antonio:

> He was indeed the duke, out o' th' substitution
> And executing th' outward face of royalty
> With all prerogative...
> To have no screen between this part he play'd

And him he play'd it for, he needs will be
Absolute Milan.[26]

Then comes the tale of the betrayal. Alonso the King of Naples, who aided and abetted him, is also not free of blame. He too is greedy for power for he agreed to help Antonio only if Milan became his subject-state, paying tribute:

To give him annual tribute, do him homage,
Subject his coronet to his crown and bend
The dukedom yet unbow'd.[27]

Thus the two of them deposed Prospero and threw him out of the kingdom. Yet Prospero and Miranda did not die as they had hoped. Instead, father and daughter, "by divine providence," arrive at this island. Here Prospero becomes guilty, perhaps all unawares, of doing the same thing as his brother had done, in a far more mild manner. In other words, he takes the island for his own dominion, neglecting the native inhabitant, that is, Caliban. At least, Caliban regards him as an usurper and says:

This island's mine by Sycorax my mother
Which thou tak'st from me. . . . .
For I am all the subjects that you have
What first was mine own kingdom.[28]

Prospero thus is guilty of the same crime from which he himself is suffering and of which he was initially a victim.

Again, when we come to the two murder-plots, the same struggle for power is to be seen. Sebastian is tempted by Antonio to kill his own brother, and he agrees to do it:

One stroke
Shall free thee from the tribute which thou payest,
And I the king shall love thee.[29]

Sebastian, like Antonio, is willing to kill his own brother, thus committing both high treason and fratricide, so he may become the king.

The plot of the lesser characters to kill Prospero is centred around the same thirst for power. Caliban gets the attention of Stephano by telling him how Prospero had usurped the island which rightfully belonged to him. It is noticeable that he does not want to rule the island. He will be content to serve Stephano if Prospero is killed. Stephano is only too willing:

> Monster, I will kill this man. His daughter and I will be king and queen—save our graces!—and Trinculo and thyself shall be viceroys.[30]

This plot, like the first one, is nipped in the bud, but it is perfectly true that Shakespeare has presented these characters as persons who are motivated by the lust for power to such an extent that they are ready to kill. Prospero is an exception, for though he usurps Caliban's kingdom, yet at the end he renounces all his supernatural powers, retaining only that which is rightfully his, the duchy of Milan. It is only fitting that he should be the most important character in the play:

> Since the major theme of the play is usurpation, it is apt that Prospero should be the centre of the action and its controller.[31]

(g) The Theme of Transformation

Shakespeare, in these last romances, shows a gradual transformation of the characters. Such transformations occur in the earlier plays as well, but this theme emerges much more strongly in the last plays. Each of the characters in this play undergoes some kind of transformation or other, and usually the transformation is a positive one, most of the time having deeply philosophical, if not religious, implications. It has been highlighted by modern critics:

> In the final comedies involving sin and sacrificial forgiveness...character development is concerned with a transformation of values.[32]

The theme of transformation is stressed from the very beginning. One can see in the second scene of Act I how Prospero has been transformed from an ivory-tower intellectual into a powerful magician and a responsible father. But this is only the beginning. More transformations in his character are still in store. He had thoughts of revenge in his heart in the past, but now these are forgotten. Instead of avenging himself, he now forgives his enemies out of his own free will:

Though with their high wrongs I am struck
to th' quick,
Yet with my nobler reason 'gainst
my fury
Do I take part. The rarer action is
In virtue than in vengeance.[33]

When the time comes to put his thoughts into action, he fulfils our expectations by forgiving his enemies even before they ask for it. This becomes the most remarkable where Antonio is concerned, for Prospero knows he will never change:

For you, most wicked sir, whom to call brother
Would even infect my mouth, I do forgive
Thy rankest fault—all of them.[34]

The full extent of his transformation, however, is to be seen when he renounces his magic powers. Here indeed he attains to the heights of true nobility. It is an unparalleled achievement not only on Prospero's part, but also on Shakespeare's part. By making Prospero abjure his magic arts, Shakespeare gives him a superhuman status, yet, at the same time, brings him back to the world of ordinary men.

The other characters in the play also undergo transformations though theirs are not so significant as that of Prospero. Alonso, for example, changes through grief for the supposed loss of his son. There had been evil in him for, conspiring with Antonio, he had invaded Milan at night, deposed Prospero and exacted tribute thereafter from the puppet-duke. Now, however, his heart has been purged of its impurities by the fire of suffering. We see a changed man in the fifth Act, who humbly asks for pardon:

Thy dukedom I resign, and do entreat
Thou pardon me my wrongs.[35]

These two are the most important transformations in the play, but the others also undergo transformations in their characters. Even Caliban, on whom Prospero's teachings had very little effect, changes into a more pleasant person when he realises his mistakes:

I'll be wise hereafter,
And seek for grace. What a thrice double ass
Was I to take this drunkard for a god.[36]

The other characters, in greater or lesser degree, also change in the play and usually the change is for the better. The only ones who do not undergo any positive change are Sebastian and Antonio. Prospero's speech makes one think that he thinks they are incapable of turning over a new leaf. The evil in them is ineradicable.

Besides these, there are many other themes in the play. The themes of reconciliation, of revenge, of self-discovery, of "ethical control over passion", of learning, of ingratitude and betrayal, and many others have been found to have been expounded in this play. It is a very complex play and the great wealth of interpretations emphasizes this complexity.

REFERENCES

1. Act I, sc. ii, *l.* 245, pp. 14-15.
2. Dowden, E., *The Serenity of The Tempest,* in Palmer, *op. cit*, pp. 74-75.
3. Act III, sc. i, *ll.* 4-7, p. 48.
4. Act III, sc. i, *ll.* 64-66, p. 50.
5. Act III, sc. i, *ll.* 83-84, p. 51.
6. The Epilogue, *ll.* 321-27, p. 88.
7. Act II, sc. i, *ll.* 146-49, p. 33.
8. Act II, sc. i, *ll.* 156-61, p. 33.
9. Murry, J.M., *Shakespeare's Dream,* in Palmer, *op. cit*, pp. 111-12.
10. Act I, sc. ii, *ll.* 74-77, p. 7.
11. Act I, sc. ii, *ll.* 89-93, p. 8.
12. Tillyard, E.M.W., *The Tragic Pattern,* in Palmer, *op. cit*, p. 129.
13. Act V, sc. i, *ll.* 310-11, p. 87.
14. The Epilogue, Act V, *ll.* 333-36, p. 88.
15. Spencer, T., *Shakespeare and the Nature of Man*, New York, Macmillan, 1942, p. 199.
16. Kermode, F., *Introduction to the Tempest,* in Palmer, *op. cit.*, p. 179.
17. *Ibid.*, p. 187.
18. Act V, sc. i, *ll.* 188-90, p. 71.
19. Zimbardo, Rose L., *Form and Disorder in The Tempest,* in Palmer, *op. cit.*, p. 237.

20. Act V, sc. i, *ll.* 11-12, p. 76.
21. Act V, sc. i, *ll.* 104-05, p. 79.
22. Act V, sc. i, *ll.* 114-15, p. 79.
23. Palmer, *op. cit*, p. 239.
24. Act V, sc. i, *ll.* 294-96, p. 86.
25. Kott, J., *Prospero's Staff*, in Palmer, *op. cit*, p. 246.
26. Act I, sc. ii, *ll.* 102-09, pp. 8-9.
27. Act I, sc. ii, *ll.* 112-14, p. 9.
28. Act I, sc. ii, *ll.* 331-42, pp. 18-19.
29. Act II, sc. ii, *ll.* 289-91, p. 39.
30. Act III, sc. ii, *ll.* 104-06, p. 56.
31. Andretta, R.A., *Shakespeare's Romances*, New Delhi, Vikas Pub. House Pvt. Ltd., 1981, p. 84.
32. Champion, L.S., *The Evolution of Shakespeare's Comedies: A Study in Dramatic Perspectives*, Harvard Univ. Press, 1973, p. 10.
33. Act V, sc. i, *ll.* 25-28, p. 76.
34. Act V, sc. i, *ll.* 130-32, p. 80.
35. Act V, sc. i, *ll.* 118-19, p. 79.
36. Act V, sc. i, *ll.* 294-96, p. 86.

7

The Major Characters

(a) Shakespeare's Characters

Much of the excellence of a play depends upon the dramatist's ability to portray characters, and our poet stands unrivalled in this sphere. His characters are more than realistic and three-dimensional human beings, for they often get the symbolic dimension of representing basic qualities of humanity. They thus become universal figures. Some dramatists like Marlowe depict the central figures with great expertise but other characters remain shadowy, neglected figures. Shakespeare, except in his early works, depicts all characters, however minor they might be, in such a way that they attain an individual essence of their own.

Setting all this aside, it has to be remembered that it is he who has given more memorable dramatic characters than any other writer. The great tragic heroes, Macbeth, Hamlet, etc., the heroines of the comedies like Rosalind, Viola and many, many others, are immortal dramatic characters. Other dramatists have given one or two such figures, but Shakespeare has given an entire gallery of highly individualised portraits.

An important aspect of his art of characterization is that he never stood still. There is continuous development in his career to the very end. His understanding of human beings developed as he himself grew older, and so did his capacity of delineating characters. He came to a position of having a great insight into the human psyche, the depth and the infinite complexity of the mind. In this respect Pope's comment made more than two centuries ago, still holds true:

> His characters are so much Nature herself that 'tis a sort of injury to call them by so distant a name as copies of her.[1]

A survey of the development of his dramatic career shows that this expertise was not there in the beginning. It was acquired slowly and surely but also painstakingly. In the first phase he was learning his art and the characters show signs of immaturity. The witty lords in *Love's Labour's Lost* are hardly to be distinguished from each other, though even at this early stage Lord Berowne stands out. There is a pair of lovers in *A Midsummer Night's Dream* who, again, can hardly be distinguished from each other. Yet even here there is the character of Bottom, a highly individualised portrayal. Another such memorable character in the early phase of his career is King Richard III, the central figure in the play named after him.

The second phase of his career shows more conscious artistry in every field, including that of characterization. The characters of this time already show understanding of human nature. It is here that we have the important male figures of the Chronicle plays and the charming heroines of the golden comedies. These four heroines, Rosalind of *As You Like It*, Beatrice of *Much Ado About Nothing*, Portia of *The Merchant of Venice* and Viola of *Twelfth Night* become so important that their male counterparts are cast into shade. The only male character of these comedies who towers above everyone else is Shylock, to whom Shakespeare has given an individuality which is truly enviable.

It is in the third stage of his development that he gives us the great male characters. The four great tragedies and the problem comedies were written at this time, presenting a world in which evil predominates. The great figures of Hamlet, Macbeth, Lear and Othello were created at this time. It is not that we have no memorable female characters. Lady Macbeth will be an outstanding figure at any time. Such characters are much more than merely realistic, for they have become universal figures.

In the Last Romances (to which category our play belongs) we find a different kind of human beings. These characters obtain an almost religious dimension. As has been seen in the chapter on the themes of these plays (Chapter 6, *supra*), the chief character undergoes a spiritual journey. Being a fallible human being, he commits sins. Then he spends long years of suffering and repentance which purifies his character. His sins are forgiven in the end. Meanwhile a younger generation of purer and more innocent nature has grown to maturity. This is what happens in the play under discussion. Here all the characters, while being masterfully-delineated individuals, have symbolic aspects as well.

It should be remembered that Shakespeare, though he had astounding originality, did not create his characters entirely out of his own imagination. Contemporary customs and contemporary stage-conventions were there to provide a base, as well as classical rules and examples. Rules for characterization had been laid down by Aristotle and expounded by later critics. Practical examples were to be found in the classical comedies and tragedies. As has been pointed out earlier (see Chapter 3, Life and Works, *supra*), Shakespeare had studied classical plays in his school-days, the plays of Plautus, Terence and Seneca. There were also many other works that defined and gave examples of characters. Some such books are: Newton's *The Touchstone of Complexions,* Hall's *Characters of Virtues and Vices*, Sir Thomas Overbury's *Characters*, etc. When in need of a certain kind of character, the dramatists could turn to these.

Theophrastus gives more than a hundred of such character-sketches. The tradition had been started by Aristotle who gave a list of six characters in his *Nichomachaean Ethics*. In *Poetics* he also laid down certain rules, applicable to all dramatic characters, irrespective of the fact whether they are tragic characters or comic ones. There are four traits all characters should have: (a) Proportion, (b) Appropriateness, (c) Realism and (d) Consistency.

The first of these, the quality of Proportion, has two implications. The moral intention underlying any action or speech must be good.

> Any speech or action that manifests moral purpose of any kind will be expressive of character: the character will be good if the purpose is good.[2]

This goodness, however, is a relative goodness, differing with characters of different classes. If a servant refrains from theft then he is good, but the same quality does not signify anything serious in a gentleman. This concept was later extended to include the possibility of evil in a character. Goodness and evil must both exist in a character.

The second quality is Appropriateness or Propriety. A character should act or speak in accordance with the kind of person that he is:

> There is a type of manly valour; but valour in a woman, or unscrupulous cleverness, is inappropriate.[3]

Shakespeare always follows this rule. Prospero is a wise and powerful mage. His actions and speeches are always dignified. The jester and the drunken butler are low-class characters and therefore they do not have dignity. They provoke laughter.

The third quality demanded by Aristotle is that the character should be true to life. Aristotle carefully points out that this quality is different from goodness and propriety, but he does not say much else about it. Shakespeare's characters, indeed, are always true to life. Their actions and speeches, given the situation, never go against what may be perfectly natural and realistic. When, in the log-carrying scene Miranda offers to carry the logs, it is perfectly realistic. When Ferdinand refuses to let her do so, that too is quite natural.

The fourth quality of consistency is, perhaps, the most important of all, for this demands that the character must remain true to his own inner nature. The best examples of this in *The Tempest* are Antonio and Sebastian. There is so much ingrained evil in them that they do not undergo repentance and change as Alonso does. Shakespeare knew that such people do not and cannot change. It would be inconsistent to change them for the better, so they remain the same. The only character who does undergo a total change is Alonso, but this is made acceptable by making him undergo the terrible experience of losing his only son. We also know that Prospero himself has changed, but this change has taken place over twelve long years. The play itself, which covers the span of only a few hours, does not present any drastic change in him. When the play opens we see him already as a changed person.

There are, thus, two important factors to be noted in the delineation of characters. On one hand there are the classical rules and on the other the practical sketches given by the classical and contemporary writers. Shakespeare as well as the other writers of the age had easy access to these sources. Yet it is Shakespeare who has given us characters who have become part of our lives, and more of them than any other writer. It is not the case, either, that he defied the age-old rules and conventions. Very often he did follow the rules and the conventions of the time. Working within these confines, he adapted them to suit his requirements. Henri Fluchère highlights this feature:

> It is equally undeniable that, allowing for his own peculiar genius, he conforms with the accepted conventions of character-drawing as with other conventions.[4]

When we turn to the characters of this play, several features strike us at once. The most obvious of them is that the range of characters in this play is far wider than in any of his other plays. In the other plays he does cover a vast range of characters, from kings to servants, but *The Tempest* differs from them in this—here he takes up not only human characters, but non-human ones also. As far as the human characters go, the range is extremely wide, for there are kings, courtiers, servants, sailors, etc., but he goes far beyond humanity. He rises to superhuman ones and reaches down to the subhumans. Ariel belongs to the former and Caliban to the latter. This feature has been a well-known aspect of the play, summed up by D.J. Palmer:

> It ranges through the scale of creatures from a subhuman brute to the spirits of the air, between which extremes the mechanicals, the courtiers, the members of royalty, children and their fathers, each occupy an appropriate station.[5]

Keeping in mind this extraordinary range and variety, the characters of *The Tempest* have been classified into four distinct groups by G. Wilson Knight. (1) Prospero, Ariel and Caliban, because of their symbolic, preternatural qualities come within one group. (2) Alonso and his party make up a group of persons who (except for Gonzalo) are in one way or another the guilty ones. (3) Stephano and Trinculo make up the group of comic characters. (4) Ferdinand and Miranda make up the last group. This grouping accounts for everyone but the two sailors, that is the Shipmaster and the Boatswain have been overlooked. Not only does G. Wilson Knight divide the characters into these groups, he also grades them according to importance. Thus according to him the three characters of the first group are called "these three main persons",[6] and Alonso and his party are "subsidiary persons". He considers Ferdinand and Miranda to be "representative of beauty and virtuous youth as drawn in former plays".[7] He makes these divisions even more clear:

> Except for Prospero, Ariel and Caliban, the people scarcely exist in their own right. The real drama concerns the actions and interplay of our three major persons with the natural, human and spiritual powers.[8]

This is G. Wilson Knight's interpretation. For the convenience of the students, however, Ferdinand and Miranda will also be considered in the present work as major characters. They are the ones who justify the label of Romance given to the play. They not only represent the theme of love, but they also help to illustrate the theme of regeneration and continuation which is common to all these four plays.

It has also been pointed out that all the characters of this play are interdependent. None of them can stand alone. In *Twelfth Night*, for example, Malvolio is an entirely independent character, but in *The Tempest* each character depends upon another or all the others. Prospero, the great magician, has to depend on Caliban for the menial tasks that have to be carried out for existing on the island. More than this, he depends on Ariel to carry out all the magical tasks. He needs Ariel at every step—raising the storm, safekeeping of the ship and the crew, separating Ferdinand from the others and bringing him, the feast, the masque, bringing all the characters to his cell in an enchanted condition and, finally, raising the right kind of wind so that everyone may reach Naples safely. In fact, Prospero is totally dependent on him. Ariel, on the other hand, depends upon him to gain his liberty. This kind of interdependence is at force with each character. As R. Andretta has pointed out:

> This dependence, whether for good or for evil, serves as an ironic comment on Prospero's initial isolation and immersion in his studies.[9]

The characters of the play, thus, present some features that are unique to this play. The vast range covered by the poet is one of them. Added to this is the fact that in this play there are at least two characters who are totally unique: Prospero and Caliban. Prospero is the only Shakespearean character who has power over supernatural spirits and Caliban is the only one who is half-human. It is also one of the rare plays of Shakespeare in which it is difficult to know what is the status of some of the characters—major or minor. For the sake of convenience, Prospero, Ariel, Caliban, Ferdinand and Miranda will be considered as major characters. Alonso, Antonio, Sebastian, Gonzalo, Stephano, Trinculo and the others will be considered as minor ones. The characters of the Masque, Iris, Ceres and Juno, will not be considered in this section as they do not really belong to the actual world of living characters.

(b) Prospero

Prospero is not only the most powerful figure in *The Tempest*, he is one of the most important characters in the whole of Shakespeare's works. It has often been the tendency of critics and readers to identify the author of a work with the hero of that work. Shakespeare's personality is so elusive that it discourages the readers to identify him with his heroes. It would be absurd, for example, to say that he resembles Lear or Othello or Duke Orsino. Prospero, however, is the one character who has encouraged critics to think that Shakespeare has partially identified himself with this character. Prospero's farewell to his magic is specially taken to be Shakespeare's farewell to the world of theatre.

Prospero is presented as a character who has attained great mental development through suffering. He was a born intellectual, immersed in his studies, oblivious of the outer world. This would not have been of much importance in others but it assumed great importance in his case because he was the Duke of Milan. Being the sovereign ruler of a place, he had a highly responsible position and he chose to neglect his duties. He left the governance of the kingdom to his brother and himself indulged in his intellectual leanings. There are many kings who neglect their royal duties, plunging themselves in the world of luxurious living and are condemned for this neglect. Shakespeare shows that the neglect of duties for the sake of studies is also to be condemned, for this is no less of a self-indulgence than indulging in luxurious life, or in amorous pursuits. Prospero, looking back at this part of his life, severely condemns it on two accounts, first because he neglected his own duties and secondly because this offered temptation to his brother:

> I thus neglecting worldly ends, all dedicated
> To closeness and the bettering of my mind
> . . . . in my false brother,
> Awak'd an evil nature, and my trust
> Like a good parent, did beget of him
> A falsehood in its contrary as great
> As my trust was.[10]

In other words, he had not been a good administrator and had brought his misfortunes upon himself by reposing trust on a person who was unworthy of it. The twelve years of enforced exile on the island, with the care of a helpless infant brought about a great change in him. Not only did he come to realise his own faults, he also came to realise the special importance of repentance leading to forgiveness.

In the island he showed his potentialities for development, not as a scholar, but as a human being, even if we set aside his ability to give practical application of his studies—his magic. This magic helped to set Ariel free and helped them survive on the island. But, apart from that, he was the father and the mother, the teacher and the mentor of Miranda. Just as Miranda was totally dependent on him for her very survival, so, in a less practical way, was he dependent on Miranda to help him survive his trials:

> O, a cherubin
> Thou wast that did preserve me
> . . . . which rais'd in me
> An undergoing stomach to bear up
> Against what should ensue.[11]

Not only did the baby Miranda help him to carry on with the business of living, but, as time went on, he developed from a father into a teacher as well, for he realised that the full responsibility of her mental and physical well-being depended on him:

> Have I, thy schoolmaster, made thee more profit
> Than other princes can that have more time
> For vainer hours, and tutors not so careful.[12]

Now that, after twelve years, Miranda has reached a marriageable age, it is his duty to see to her future security and he does this most consummately well by having Ferdinand brought to her.

It is not merely that he is careful of his daughter's well-being, but of those too who, unlike her, are not flesh of his flesh and blood of his blood. He sets Ariel free by his superior magic though he retains his services. What is more praiseworthy, he takes the unprepossessing Caliban under his wing and tries to educate him. Caliban could not talk and Prospero it was who taught him to do so. Caliban himself acknowledges this when he says:

> When thou cam'st first
> Thou strok'dst me and mad'st much of me;
> Wouldst give me
> Water with berries in't; and teach me how
> To name the bigger light and the less.[13]

What is more, he had allowed Caliban to sleep with him and Miranda in the same cave. Caliban, however, was not fully human and could be taught only to a certain extent, beyond which he could not take in any more. Prospero realises this:

> On whose nature
> Nurture can never stick; on whom my pains
> Humanely taken, all, all lost, quite lost.[14]

Caliban tried to violate Miranda and thereafter Prospero ceased to care for him. He had, however, to his credit, tried to educate and civilize Caliban at first. This is particularly praiseworthy when one remembers that he had been a king who was so intellectual that he had withdrawn into the ivory tower of his intellectual pursuits. The island had, by separating him from his kingdom, made him more aware of his duties. As a person he had developed into a good father and a good teacher who had tried to educate even a being who was not fully human.

Prospero, when we see him as the sovereign lord of the island, has attained an almost superhuman status, not only through his powerful magic but also through the force of his highly mature personality. G. Wilson Knight, indeed, calls him the Shakespearean superman. There are many interpretations and analyses of his character. One such interpretation is that he is more or less an autobiographical figure. It was the poet Campbell who first suggested this view and many later critics accepted it:

> Prospero, who controls this comprehensive Shakespearean world, automatically reflects Shakespeare himself.[15]

It is specially with reference to his renunciation of his magical powers that this interpretation is thought to be relevant. Prospero has always been in full control of the situation and in Act V he decides to go back to Milan to lead an ordinary life. Therefore he renounces his magic powers. This power had extended over nature, over the elements and also over superhuman creatures like Ariel. He draws a magic circle with his wand, summons all the spirits and gives a catalogue of the different kinds of powers he had. Then in a magnificent, unequalled gesture he voluntarily renounces these powers now:

> I'll break my staff,
> Bury it certain fathoms in the earth,
> And deeper than did ever plummet sound,
> I'll drown my book.[16]

This gesture gains in grandeur because it is totally voluntary and points to the height of maturity that Prospero has reached to be able to relinquish this wonderful power willingly:

> ...the consecrated estimate of Prospero's surrender of his magic robe and staff [can be seen] as a figure for Shakespeare's own self-despoilment, his considered purpose, at this date, of future silence.[17]

The same idea has been repeated by others:

> I find it impossible to deny that Prospero is, to some extent, an imaginary paradigm of Shakespeare himself in his function as a poet.[18]

There are many other interpretations of his character even if this autobiographical one is not taken into account. His character has four aspects—the magician, the ruler, the scholar and the man. All these four different aspects have their own functions and relevance and unite to create the wonderful character that he is. Analysing from this point of view and keeping the four different aspects in mind, the development of the character from a withdrawn, negligent ruler into a man who has learnt the value of repentance and forgiveness is clearly seen. It is his ability to forgive his enemies and renounce his powers that gives a sublime quality to his character. Not only does he give up his powers without being asked, but he also forgives his enemies voluntarily. The memory of his wrong is still green in his mind, but he does not dwell on revenge. If he can make his enemies repent and then forgive them it will be revenge enough for him. This highly Christian sentiment is clearly expressed in the fifth Act. Ariel has told him how the culprits whose guilty conscience have awakened are repenting of their misdeeds, and he responds in a manner worthy of him:

Though with their high wrongs I am struck
to th'quick
Yet with nobler reasons 'gainst my fury
Do I take part. The rarer action is
In virtue than in vengeance. They
being penitent,
The sole drift of my purpose doth extend
Not a frown further.[19]

This is no mere high-sounding and insincere self-glorification. His practice is as noble as his speech, for when he sees the culprits he freely forgives them, even before he is asked. Thus he embraces Alonso:

I embrace thy body
And to thee and thy company I bid
A hearty welcome.[20]

Turning to Antonio, whose sin is such that it can hardly be forgiven, he says:

For you, most wicked sir, whom to call brother
Would even infect my mouth, I do forgive
Thy rankest fault—all of them.[21]

These two actions of his, renunciation and forgiveness, give a superhuman sublimity to his character that no other Shakespearean hero has.

(c) Prince Ferdinand

Ferdinand, the romantic hero of the play, is more the vision of an ideal young lover than an individual human being. He is also the ideal heir to a kingdom, gentle by nature and manner, obedient and sincere, a young man with high moral principles and a loving son. These virtues are paralleled by his very handsome physical appearance. When Miranda sees him for the first time he is like a divine being to her:

I might call him
A thing divine, for nothing natural
I ever saw so noble.[22]

The log-bearing scene shows him at his best. He is deeply in love with Miranda, in the chivalric Petrarchan manner. He has taken on the task of carrying the logs like a knightly duty. It is a task very much below his dignity, yet his point of view gives the task the dignity and romance that is always accorded to chivalric love:

> This my mean task
> Would be as heavy to me, as odious, but
> The mistress which I serve quickens what's dead,
> And makes my labours pleasures.[23]

This is the authentic attitude of a chivalrous lover. Thus when Miranda comes he responds in the manner expected of such a lover. When Miranda wants him to sit down and rest while she does his work, he replies vehemently:

> No, precious creature
> I had rather crack my sinews, break my back
> Than you should such dishonour undergo.[24]

He declares his admiration for her in such terms as would melt the heart of any girl:

> Admir'd Miranda,
> Indeed the top of admiration, worth
> What's dearest to the world! . . . . . .
> . . . . But you, O you,
> So perfect and so peerless, are created
> Of every creature's best.[25]

Later when Miranda artlessly asks him if he loves her or not, his answer rings true in each syllable.

> I
> Beyond all limit of what else—i' th' world—
> Do love, prize and honour you.[26]

This is the authentic, true and enduring love that sanctifies life. When Miranda asks him whether he is willing to marry her, he promises marriage with promptness and sincerity thus:

> Ay, with a heart as willing
> As bondage e'er of freedom. Here's my hand.[27]

The impression that Ferdinand creates of innocence and sincerity is reinforced in the betrothal scene, the first scene of the fourth Act. He accepts Prospero's explanation of his trial without any question and receives Miranda with dignity and grace. He does not speak much in this scene, except to accept, with due grace, Prospero's strictures on pre-marriage intimacy with Miranda. Later, in the last scene he is dignified and controlled when he meets his father and introduces Miranda to him. In every instance, as a matter of fact, he acts exactly as is expected of him.

These, however, are superficial features. At a deeper level he becomes a far more important, almost symbolic, figure. Together with Miranda, he represents the new younger and purer generation which will carry on the flame of life. As has been pointed out by Middleton Murry *The Tempest* deals with the theme of the evil done by the elder generation being obliterated by the next generation. It is Ferdinand who, together with Miranda, perform this important function (*vide* Chapter 6, The Major Themes, *Supra*). Ferdinand, therefore, is the representative, not only of a younger generation, but of the humanity, pure and free of sin, which will build up a brave new world. He is the god of spring who brings new life after winter.

Referring to the theme of Nature and Nurture as dealt within the play, it has also been pointed out that Ferdinand is the best illustration of the practical application of this theme. On one hand there is nature which, though it gives a life of purity and innocence, lacks sophistication. Nature, therefore, when cultivated in the proper way, *i.e.* nurtured, gives forth the best results. This is what we have in Ferdinand. He is a man who is gentle, brave and obedient by nature. Proper education and training has made him a noble, polished and sincere young man who is the ideal one for a future monarch. He is a courteous prince, the living example of the union of nature and nurture at its best:

> He has had a good education and excellent upbringing and his nature seems to have responded favourably to them.[28]

This question of nurture (*i.e.* education and upbringing) becomes even more clear when he is contrasted with Caliban of whom Prospero says:

A devil, a born devil, on whose nature
Nurture can never stick; on whom my pains,
Humanely taken, all, all lost, quite lost.[29]

Ferdinand and Caliban thus serve as foils to each other. All these features of his character combine to make him a fine upstanding young man whose soul is pure and innocent. One implication of this purity becomes clear when it is seen that he can hear the unearthly music of the island which no one else (except Gonzalo) can hear. His soul is fine enough and sensitive enough to be capable of hearing one of the best songs of Shakespeare, "Full fathom five". Not only does he hear this music but his soul also responds to it, becoming calm under its soothing influence. It is only when he has become serene and is at harmony with the spirit of the island that he is allowed to see Miranda and love her.

It is also a pertinent point that the theme of love is presented through him. This love is not only an idealistic chivalric love; it also conforms to the Renaissance ideal of love by being chaste and controlled. Ferdinand, when being instructed to be chaste, not only accepts it as being perfectly natural but relates chastity to moral values when he declares that he hopes:

For quiet days and fair issues and long life
With such love as 't is now.[30]

This love is the kind of love approved by society and religion and it is Ferdinand who is the embodiment of it. This aspect is to be found only in Ferdinand among the romantic heroes of the four Last Romances.

(d) Ariel

Ariel, a creature of fire and air, is a wondrous creation of Shakespeare. He is not a unique creature like Caliban, for he has a fore-runner in Puck of *A Midsummer Night's Dream*. He is a being who has great supernatural powers and is not subject to human limitations or moral standards. Yet this much is known: ignoble or mean thoughts and actions are inimical to him, for he had refused to do the bidding of the witch Sycorax:

And for thou wast a spirit too delicate
To act her earthy and abhorred commands
Refusing her grand hests.[31]

Sycorax punished him by splitting open a pine tree and confining him there. She died without having set him free, for she was not a powerful enough magician for that. When Prospero arrived at the island he had the power to set him free and he did so, but he retained Ariel's services. Ariel, thus, is not as free as he would like to be. He still has to do Prospero's biddings and he yearns to be totally free.

Before Prospero is to set him free, however, he has to perform certain tasks. It is easily to be seen that all the magical effects that Prospero produces are actually performed by Ariel. His tasks begin even before the play does, with the raising of the tempest, and go on even after the play ends, with the safe ending of Prospero's sea journey. In between come all the numerous deeds that take the action forward and bring the play to a happy conclusion. Prospero himself does not perform any magical deed. He is the agent and Ariel is the instrument.

The supernatural powers of Ariel range from complete control over the elements to equally effective control over his own form. He brings about the tempest, thus influencing the elements of air and water, and also appears as a flame of fire. He thus has control over three elements and Caliban is intimately related to the element of earth, which is distasteful to Ariel. Not only did Ariel appear to the men in the ship as an extraordinary kind of lightning, but he also appeared at different places at the same time:

Sometimes I'd divide
And burn in many places; on the topmast,
The yards and bowsprit would I flame distinctly,
Then meet and join.[32]

It is quite clear that when performing this task he had enjoyed doing it. The fact that he had total control over his own airy form is evident in that he can "divide" himself and appear at several places at one and the same time. Moreover, he can be visible and invisible at will, for in many scenes he remains invisible to the ship's party. He also assumes whatever form he likes. He is told, for example, to take the form of a sea-nymph in the first Act and he immediately does so:

> Go make thyself like a nymph o' th' sea
> Be subject to no sight but thine and mine, invisible
> To every eyeball else.[33]

Again, in the feast-scene, he produces an entire banquet and appears as a harpy, denounces the culprits and brings on their repentance. Then, in the masque-scene, which has been produced by him, he himself appears as one of the characters, though it is not clear which. It is as if his form, being made of air, is totally malleable and can easily change itself like the Greek god Proteus.

Added to all these powers is the power of producing music. Out of the nine songs in the play, five are sung by him. Three of them are functional songs, *i.e.*, they are sung in order to fulfil some dramatic purpose. "Come into these yellow sands" and "Full fathom five" are sung to soothe Ferdinand and bring him to Prospero, and "While you here do sleeping lie" is sung to waken Gonzalo. His last two songs "Before you can say" and "Where the bee sucks" are not sung with any such purpose in mind. The first of these is just a casual song trilled out to convince Prospero that the masque will be ready as soon as he asks for it and the second expresses his joy in anticipating his freedom. (For more information on this head see Ch. 11, Poetic Style, *infra.*)

Ariel, however, is not human either in his powers or in his attitudes. He is not subject to the emotions that men are subject to. Yet Shakespeare shows him as having become susceptible, in an indirect way, to human feelings. This is clearly conveyed when he describes the penitent sinners to Prospero, describing their pitiable state:

> Ariel : Your charm so strongly works in them
> That if you now beheld them, your affections
> Would become tender.
> Prospero : Dost thou think so, spirit?
> Ariel : Mine would sir, were I human.[34]

Though he is not human, he can yet imagine how human beings would feel. This brief passage leads us to think that it is the privilege of Ariel to bring home to Prospero certain basic Christian moral values, for, it is after listening to him that Prospero rejoins: "And mine shall". Not only here alone, in the feast-scene also he embodies moral values in the guise of an avenging fury and denounces all the sinners in a speech which is thirty lines long:

> You are three men of sin, whom Destiny
> That hath to instrument this lower world
> And what is in't, the never-surfeited sea
> Hath caused to belch you up . . . . . .
> . . . . for which foul deed
> The powers delaying, not forgetting, have
> Incens'd the seas and shores, yea all the creatures
> Against your peace.[35]

This is an important feature in which Ariel differs from Puck of *A Midsummer Night's Dream*. He has, as Hazlitt has pointed out:

> ...a fellow-feeling in the interest of
> those he is employed about.[36]

Ariel is such a creature that he calls for symbolic interpretation and many such interpretations have been given. He has been called "a personification of poetry itself". This is the opinion of G. Wilson Knight who thinks that Ariel is not only of air, fire and music but also "all Shakespeare's more volatile and aerial impressionism".[37]

The Elizabethan view of the world should also be taken into account when studying the character of Ariel. The Elizabethans believed in an elaborate system of philosophy that explained the nature of the world. There are many aspects of this world-view—religious, political, metaphyscial, etc. One such aspect is their psychological concept of man's soul. It was believed that man possessed three souls. The vegetable soul is what he shares with plants and the lower animals. The characteristics of this soul are nourishing, growing and reproducing. The second soul is the sensible soul which is what he has in common with animals. This soul governs the emotions and through them influences the actions of men and animals. The third soul is the rational which is peculiar to men only and it impels men towards intellectual actions like acquiring knowledge, indulging in speculative thinking and exercising our will. According to this interpretation Ariel represents the second kind of soul—the sensible soul. He is under the control of the rational soul of Prospero and in-turn controls the elemental world of nature. In the feast-scene he arouses the feelings of penitence and shame in the sinners. It is a characteristic feature of Ariel that he himself is free from human emotions yet, when directed by the rational soul of Prospero, he can raise emotions in other human beings. His charm lies in his being so non-human, yet so childlike. There is a primal childlike innocence and delight in him that is possible in spirits and in children only. Playfulness and this charm mark him out.

(e) Caliban

Caliban is the opposite of Ariel. Just as Ariel is a creature of air and fire, so is Caliban a creature of earth and water. He is non-human, or, at most, but half-human, for though his mother, the witch Sycorax was a human, yet his father was a devil. Prospero addresses him thus:

> Thou poisonous slave, got by the devil himself
> Upon thy wicked dam.[38]

He is non-human by nature as well as by physical appearance. He is repeatedly referred to as a monster. There are not many descriptions of his appearance but whatever there is makes it clear that he is a gross monster. The most detailed description is given by Trinculo:

> What have we here,—a man or a fish?—dead or alive? A fish, he smells like a fish; a very ancient and fish-like smell; A kind of not-of-the-newest poor-John...Legged like a man, and his fins like arms.[39]

It is clear that his very appearance is a non-human and repulsive one. Yet there is enough of the human in him to make Prospero take an interest in him at first. Caliban was not hostile to Prospero and Miranda in the beginning, nor were they hostile to him. Caliban himself acknowledges it:

> When thou cam'st first,
> Thou strok'dst me and mad'st much of me;
> Wouldst give me
> Water with berries in't; and teach me how
> To name the bigger light, and how the less
> That burn by day and night; and then I lov'd thee.[40]

But all this was twelve years ago when Caliban, it must be remembered, was a very young monster who had not learnt how to speak. Prospero and Miranda shared the same cave with him. Then in due course Caliban grew up and tried to violate Miranda which made both Prospero and Miranda turn against him. Ever since then he has been treated as a hateful monster. This, in turn, has made Caliban hostile to them so that he now curses Prospero with every breath, resenting his presence on the island.

Another source of his resentment is the fact that, before Prospero came, Caliban was the lord of the island. He considered himself to be the rightful owner of the island which he had inherited from his mother Sycorax the witch. Prospero came and overthrew him:

> This island's mine by Sycorax my mother
> Which thou tak'st from me.[41]

At present, Prospero's ill-treatment and the consciousness that he is the true owner who is treated like a slave made him hostile. Basically, however, he is good-natured and simple-hearted. There is, indeed, a childlike simplicity in him that makes Trinculo call him "a most poor, credulous monster". This simplicity makes him believe Stephano to be the Man in the Moon. He is, as a matter of fact, in great need of affection, in need of a god to worship, and so he takes Stephano for a god and kneels to him. At the end of the play, however, his eyes are opened and he realises that these are but clowns and servants, very different from truly great people. He realises the nobility of Prospero:

I'll be wise hereafter
And seek for grace. What a thrice-double ass
Was I to take this drunkard for a god
And worship this dull fool.[42]

Much, however, has to happen before he can arrive at this self-knowledge. Stephano and Trinculo, in the meantime, accept his homage and he leads them to the pleasant spots in the island and plots with them to kill Prospero. Finally he leads them to the swamp near Prospero's cell where they get themselves thoroughly dirtied. Then all three of them are brought to Prospero who strongly rebukes all of them and then follows Caliban's self-knowledge which is the best kind of Anagnorisis or self-recognition according to Aristotle. (*Vide* Ch. 9, Plot, *infra.*)

Certain features of his character should be noticed. For example, though he is but a half-human monster, still he can hear the music that is continuously washing over the island:

Sounds, and sweet airs, that give delight, and hurt not.
Sometimes a thousand twangling instruments
Will hum about mine ears; and sometimes voices.[43]

When Stephano and Trinculo sing a catch out of tune, he quickly spots the fault. Later when the two clowns put on the tawdry and glittering dress over their dirty bodies, Caliban knows that the dresses are trash. Moreover, he usually speaks in verse while Stephano and Trinculo speak in prose. These special features indicate that Shakespeare intended him to be of a finer mettle than these two figures, though he is sub-human, a monster. In fact, Coleridge finds nobility in him:

> Caliban is in some respects a noble beast: the poet has raised him far above contempt.[44]

There are many ways in which he has been contrasted with the other characters. His capacity to learn is very limited. He has learnt to speak and do menial tasks but his learning has stopped there. Prospero has been teaching both Miranda and him and thus he provides a sharp contrast to Miranda. Again, he resents the tasks that Prospero gives him and carries them out most grudgingly. Herein he provides contrast to Ferdinand who willingly performs the ignoble tasks he has been set to do. He plots the murder of Prospero just as Antonio plots the murder of Alonso. Both are unsuccessful. Most important of all, he provides a sharp contrast to Ariel who is a creature of air and fire as he is of the earth and of water. He is base and gross by nature.

Caliban is a truly unique character. Ariel has a forerunner in Puck of *A Midsummer Night's Dream* but Caliban has none, anywhere. There is no other character like him in Shakespeare. This fact had been noticed and pointed out by Dryden:

> He seems there to have created a person which was not in nature...he makes him a species of himself, begotten by an incubus on a witch.[45]

Caliban, moreover, is perhaps the only character in *The Tempest* who has no literary progenitor. He represents both the Elizabethan idea of the wild man as well as that of the savages of the New World. As a matter of fact, his name is supposed to be an anagram of the word "cannibal". Descriptions of the savages of the New World as well as those of the wild men of the Old World were to be found in many well-known travelogues of the time.

(f) Miranda

Miranda is the only female character in the play and in this she is unique. There is no other Shakespearean heroine who does not have at least a maidservant or gentlewoman to keep her company.

She is the very embodiment of purity and innocence, and this quality is so obvious in her that it has been recognised right from the very beginning. Coleridge sees her as the ideal woman:

> Of Miranda we may say, that she possesses in herself all the ideal beauties that could be imagined by the greatest poet of any age or country.[46]

Miranda is the perfect result of Nature and Nurture for she has been brought up in a totally pastoral environment and has been educated by Prospero:

Here in this island we arriv'd, and here
Have I, thy schoolmaster made thee more profit
Than other princes can that have more time
For vainer hours, and tutors not so careful.[47]

Prospero has inculcated in her the virtues of obedience, modesty and purity and she has an inborn gentleness and pity that becomes clear in the expository scene when she sees the mariners tossing about in the stormy sea. We also come to know that she is kind and friendly by nature as she taught Caliban:

I pitied thee
Took pains to make thee speak, taught
thee each hour
One thing or other.[48]

Recalling happier days, Caliban tells Stephano how Miranda had shown him the Man in the Moon:

I have seen thee in her, and I do
adore thee. My mistress showed me
thee, and thy dog and thy bush.[49]

She is easily the most innocent of Shakespeare's heroines as she has never seen any man other than her father and mistakes Ferdinand for a spirit. All the usual feminine qualities that have been dormant in her heart awaken when she sees him, for she falls instantly in love with him. This love is the pure, idealistic, worshipful love of an innocent maiden. It is the true and enduring love which glorifies life. It is so strong that, for the first time she disobeys her father and visits Ferdinand in secret.

This scene, commonly known as the log-carrying scene (the first scene of Act III) is the only one in which the two lovers are alone together. Their love for each other is an idealistic, intense love in the Petrarchan tradition. Ferdinand has undertaken the job of carrying logs in the spirit of knightly chivalry, but Miranda differs from the typical female characters of such literature in that she is no disdainful lady. Instead she comes forward with sympathy for Ferdinand and offers her love in all innocence and purity:

I would not wish
Any company in the world but you;
Nor can imagination form a shape
Besides yourself to look of.[50]

She has not learnt to be coquettish or flirtatious, and is quite open in her expressions. There is also great humility in her, for hers is the true love that glorifies the beloved and thinks itself unworthy:

Hence, bashful cunning,
And prompt me, plain and holy innocence!
I am your wife if you will marry me
If not, I'll die your maid. To be your fellow
You may deny me, but I'll be your servant
Whether you will, or no.[51]

In the betrothal-scene she does not speak at all which is quite in keeping with Elizabethan ideas of maidenly modesty, but Shakespeare has given her one of his best-known passages:

How many goodly creatures are there here!
How beauteous mankind is! O brave new world!
That has such people in't![52]

The character of Miranda is, indeed, extremely simple from one point of view, and from another it is so complex that it rises to symbolic heights. On the face of it she is the pure-hearted heroine of the pastoral tradition—a maiden untouched by worldly corruption, but this is only one side of this enchanting figure. As her name itself indicates, she is a truly wonderful creature worthy of admiration, for she is unique among Shakespeare's heroines. This aspect has been lauded again and again:

> Such is the inexhaustible plenty of our poet's inventions that he has exhibited another character in this play, entirely his own: that of the lovely and innocent Miranda.[53]

This remark is fully justified because she is not modelled on any or more than one definite female characters to be found in the sources he used. As a matter of fact *The Tempest* is one of the plays of Shakespeare which does not have any former play or story as its source. (*Vide* Ch. 9 *infra.*)

It is not that she has no forerunners among Shakespeare's own heroines. She has much in common with the other three heroines of the last romances—Imogen, Marina and Perdita. Like them, we will see, she too is the possessor of the two qualities of innocence and purity. The difference between her and the others lies in the fact that in her these qualities are far more intensified. Indeed her innocence, from a negative point of view, can be called an unnatural ignorance, for she has not seen any human being except her father. This is an unnatural state of affairs. She cannot, really, be called a child of Nature as Perdita of *The Winter's Tale* can be. Perdita too has been brought up in the lap of nature, away from urban sophistication, but she has been surrounded by other persons. Miranda, on the other hand, has been carefully brought up by Prospero, who has lavished on her all the love and care that a man can give. So she is a combination of the best that Nature and Nurture can produce.

Miranda, indeed, from the very beginning, is more of a symbolic figure than a realistic individual. She and Ferdinand together symbolise pure and enduring love. They also represent the new generation of uncorrupted youth and beauty on whom the future of humanity rests. Miranda in herself, symbolising purity and innocence as she does, is a character extremely difficult to delineate, in a credible manner. Shakespeare has struck a delicate balance in depicting her. As E.M.W. Tillyard has pointed out:

> Had she been more weakly drawn, she would have been insignificant, had she been drawn more strongly, she would have interfered with the unifying dominance of Prospero.[54]

REFERENCES

1. Quoted by Fluchère, Henri, *op. cit.*, p. 131.
2. Butcher, S.H., *Aristotle's Theory of Poetry and Fine Art* with a critical Text Translation of *The Poetics*, New Delhi, Kalyani Pubs., 1981. Ch. XV, p. 53.
3. *Ibid.*
4. Fluchère, H., *op. cit.*, p. 136.
5. Palmer, D.J., *op. cit.*, p. 16.

6. Knight, G. Wilson, *The Shakespearian Superman*, in Palmer, *op. cit.*, p. 139.
7. *Ibid.*, p. 148.
8. *Ibid.*
9. Andretta, R., *op. cit.*, p. 90.
10. Act I, sc. ii, *ll.* 89-96, p. 8.
11. Act I, sc. ii, *ll.* 152-58, p. 11.
12. Act I, sc. ii, *ll.* 172-74, p. 11.
13. Act I, sc. ii, *ll.* 332-35, p. 18.
14. Act IV, sc. i, *ll.* 188-90, p. 71.
15. Knight, G.W., *op. cit.*, p. 148.
16. Act V, sc. i, *ll.* 54-56, p. 77.
17. James, Henry, *Introduction to The Tempest*, in Palmer, *op. cit.*, p. 88.
18. Murry, J.M., *op. cit.*, p. 110.
19. Act V, sc. i, *ll.* 25-30, p. 76.
20. Act V, sc. i, *ll.* 109-11, p. 79.
21. Act V, sc. i, *ll.* 130-32, p. 80.
22. Act I, sc. ii, *ll.* 418-20, p. 21.
23. Act III, sc. i, *ll.* 4-7, p. 48.
24. Act III, sc. i, *ll.* 45-27, p. 49.
25. Act III, sc. i, *ll.* 37-48, p. 50.
26. Act III, sc. i, *ll.* 71-73, pp. 50-51.
27. Act III, sc. i, *ll.* 87-89, p. 51.
28. Andretta, R.A., *op. cit.*, p. 85.
29. Act IV, sc. i, *ll.* 188-90, p. 71.
30. Act IV, sc. i, *ll.* 24-25, p. 63.
31. Act I, sc. ii, *ll.* 272-74, p. 16.
32. Act I, sc. ii, *ll.* 190-201, p. 12.
33. Act I, sc. ii, *ll.* 301-03, p. 17.
34. Act V, sc. i, *ll.* 17-20, p. 76.
35. Act III, sc. ii, *ll.* 53-75, p. 61.
36. Hazlitt, *op. cit.*, p. 70.
37. Knight, G.W., *op. cit.*, p. 136.
38. Act I, sc. ii, *ll.* 319-20, p. 18.
39. Act II, sc. ii, *ll.* 19-33, pp. 41-42.
40. Act I, sc. ii, *ll.* 332-36, p. 18.
41. Act I, sc. ii, *ll.* 331-32, p. 18.

42. Act V, sc. i, *ll.* 294-97, p. 86.
43. Act III, sc. iii, *ll.* 134-36, p. 57.
44. Coleridge, *An Analysis of Act I,* in Palmer, *op. cit.,* p. 58.
45. Dryden, *The Character of Caliban*, in Palmer, *op. cit.,* p. 34.
46. Coleridge, *op. cit.*, p. 60.
47. Act I, sc. ii, *ll.* 171-74, p. 11.
48. Act I, sc. ii, *ll.* 352-54, p. 19.
49. Act II, sc. ii, *ll.* 137-38, p. 45.
50. Act III, sc. i, *ll.* 54-57, p. 50.
51. Act III, sc. i, *ll.* 81-86, p. 51.
52. Act V, sc. i, *ll.* 181-84, p. 82.
53. Warton, Joseph, *Remarks on the Creation of Characters*, in Palmer, *op. cit.,* p. 45.
54. Tillyard, E.M.W., *op. cit.,* p. 129.

8

The Minor Characters

It is one of the many reasons behind Shakespeare's supremacy over the other dramatists of his age that he took pains over the delineations of his minor characters as well as over those of his major ones. Even though a character might come on the stage for a very short time and speak very little, Shakespeare yet depicts him or her in a convincing and concrete manner so that he or she comes forth as an individual. Many of his minor characters are delineated as carefully as the important characters of other playwrights. In the play under present discussion, Prospero is such an overwhelming personality that all other characters are cast into the shade, including the romantic hero and heroine who are usually all-important in romances. Yet it cannot be denied that, though overshadowed, they still have an identity of their own.

(a) Gonzalo

He is definitely the most important of the minor characters. He is an entirely positive character and Shakespeare takes pains to introduce him as such through Prospero's speech in the expository scene (Act I, sc. ii). He impresses us as a sensible man on his very first appearance on the stage for, instead of being angry at the Boatswain's roughness of manner, he thinks that the Boatswain is an efficient person and he will save the ship from being wrecked. Then in the second scene he is described by Prospero in glowing terms:

> A noble Neapolitan, Gonzalo,
> Out of his charity, who then being appointed

> Master of this design, did give us with
> Rich garments, linens, stuffs and necessaries.[1]

Not only did Gonzalo put all those things that would help Prospero and Miranda sustain life, but he also put in the boat books of magic that Prospero had valued more than his kingdom. This action highlights the kindly and helpful character of Gonzalo. It should be remembered here that there was no question of feudal loyalty in the services Gonzalo rendered Prospero for he was no subject of Prospero's. Prospero was the duke of Milan and Gonzalo was a Neapolitan, *i.e.*, a subject of Alonso. This stranger then, out of the generosity of his heart, helped Prospero, when his own brother betrayed him.

As the play progresses one sees the different aspects of his nature gradually coming to light. He reveals himself as a character with a good deal of common sense in the first scene, as has already been pointed out. Then in the opening scene of the second Act he tries again and again to console Alonso in his grief over the supposed loss of Ferdinand. Here Shakespeare shows him as a well-meaning but rather obtuse person who cannot realise that Alonso wants to be left in peace. Antonio and Sebastian try his patience by their inane fooling, but he bears with it. It is a significant thing that he finds the island to be a pleasant and friendly place whereas Antonio and Sebastian find it to be hostile and barren. Perhaps Shakespeare means to show that people get what they deserve. There is goodness in Gonzalo, so for him the island is fertile and pleasant, but the same island appears completely different to those characters who are evil. It is only a mature vision that can relate human characters with the world of nature in this fully convincing and poetic manner.

The high point of this scene occurs with his description of the commonwealth, his vision of Utopia. This description comprises eighteen lines, two of which are half-lines. This ideal commonwealth will uphold a state of nature in which there will be no political strife or even the supremacy of one person above everyone else. Nor will it have any kind of trade or any kind of service. The relationships of king-and-subject, master-

and-slave, buyer-and-seller, will all be abolished. There will be no warfare and no destructive weapons. No one will be forced to work in order to live, whatever nature produces for general use will be used by everyone. It will be an age of innocence and happiness. The golden age will not only have come back, it would be cast into shade:

> I would with such perfection govern, sir,
> T'excel the golden age.[2]

This is an idealistic and innocent picture, and is one of the very few instances in this play where we have a definite source from which Shakespeare obtains the initial idea (*vide* Ch. 9, Plot, *infra*). It may be too idealistic and simplistic to be a practical form of government, but if that aspect is overlooked this vision of a utopia sheds significant light on Gonzalo's character which has high-mindedness and innate goodness in it. This vision, moreover, is important because it brings the theme of life in the lap of nature into the play. It has been argued that the pastoral theme is an important theme in the play:

> Gonzalo's half-serious talk about his commonwealth serves to introduce into the play the theme of natural life in a guise more appropriate to pastoral poetry which takes a soft view of Nature.[3]

This critic points out that Antonio and Sebastian continually jeer at Gonzalo, but this does not invalidate the universal theme of the innocence of life in the lap of Nature (*vide* Chapter 6, *supra*).

There are many interpretations of his character. He has been looked upon as a typical well-meaning but rather foolish courtier:

> The faithful and garrulous old Lord Gonzalo is a blend of Polonius, Adam and Kent.[4]

Indeed Gonzalo's conversation in this scene (Act II, sc. i) does present him in this light, but it must be remembered that it is he to whom the poet has given the vision of utopia.

There are several important stages in the development of the character of Gonzalo. We see him as a sensible and pious old man in the storm-scene, then as the idealistic and cheerful courtier in the second Act. Next, in the third Act, he looks at the strange spirits spreading a feast, with tolerance and benevolence:

> Who, though they are of monstrous shape, yet note
> Their manners are more gentle-kind than of
> Our human generation you shall find
> Many, nay almost any.[5]

Later, after Ariel's terrible diatribe the guilty ones are beside themselves with terror and repentance and Gonzalo is the only one who is unperturbed. It remains for him, the seniormost courtier, to take up the reins of responsibility, and he directs the other courtiers to follow and take care of the guilty persons. He shows himself as a responsible person.

At the end of the play Shakespeare gives him a highly elevated status. He attains the status of the wise and benevolent old man whose blessings sanctify the lives of the younger generation:

> Look down, you gods,
> And on this couple drop a blessed crown;
> For it is you that have chalk'd forth the way
> which brought us hither.[6]

The character of Gonzalo, thus, though a minor one, is yet a serious one as well. He emerges as a rounded, fully developed character.

(b) Alonso

Alonso the King of Naples is socially the highest placed among the minor characters. Antonio had become the Duke of Milan only through his help and by giving him tribute. His superiority has other supporting factors also, for he is morally superior to Antonio as he is not an unmitigated villain like the latter. As far as family relationships go, he is the father of the romantic hero and would become the father-in-law of the heroine. He is a man who has the seeds of goodness dormant in his heart. The supposed loss of his son and later the accusations of Ariel awaken his sleeping conscience. It is not surprising that Prospero would realise this and freely pardon him. Yet his innate nobility, once awakened, leads him to beg forgiveness:

> Thy dukedom I resign, and do entreat
> Thou pardon me my wrongs.[7]

Again, after he sees Ferdinand and Miranda and learns that Miranda is to be his daughter-in-law he begs her pardon:

> But O, how oddly will it sound that I
> Must ask my child forgiveness![8]

It has been pointed out that he had forced his own daughter Claribel into a marriage which was distasteful to her and to that of his subjects. Sebastian roundly accuses him:

> You were kneel'd to and importun'd otherwise
> By all of us, and the fair soul herself
> Weigh'd between loathness and obedience at
> Which end o' th' beam should bow.[9]

This paints him as an unreasonable and autocratic father who misuses his parental authority. This feature has led G. Wilson Knight to compare him with other such characters in Shakespeare:

> As one of Shakespeare's many autocratic fathers and also as a king rather pathetically searching for his child, he is a distant relative of Lear. Both are purgatorial figures.[10]

His remorse and asking for pardon redeems his character. His faults are forgiven by Prospero as well as Shakespeare and he is rewarded with the recovery of his son and the gaining of a daughter-in-law like the peerless Miranda.

A less important feature of his character is that he never loses his patience with Gonzalo, or with his brother Sebastian though both of them sorely try his patience. He wants to be alone in his grief for the loss of his son, yet Gonzalo continuously irritates him by trying to console him. He does realise the good intentions of the old courtier, and is therefore not harsh with him. It is only after the fooling of Antonio and

Sebastian has gone on for some considerable stretch of time that he finally rebukes them, though quite mildly.

> You cram these words in mine ears against
> The stomach of my sense.[11]

Except for this speech of seven lines he hardly speaks in this scene, and endures the chatter of Gonzalo and the inanities of his brother patiently. This points at great forbearance and is also eloquent of his grief at the loss of his son.

(c) Antonio

This is one of the blackest villains of Shakespeare. John P. Cutts, indeed, declares:

> Sebastian and Antonio are worse than devils.[12]

He comes on the stage in the very first scene—the storm-scene, and reveals himself as a foul-mouthed, impatient character. This is in effective contrast with Gonzalo's patient and pious attitude:

> Hang, cur, hang, you whoreson insolent noisemaker![13]

He abuses the mariners who are trying their best to save the ship, calling them drunks and rascals. When we see him next in the first scene of Act II, he, along with Sebastian, spends his time jeering at Gonzalo. He is determined to undermine Gonzalo and would hardly allow him to speak, interrupting him several times. As a matter of fact he and Sebastian interrupt Gonzalo five times in just one sentence so that it takes Gonzalo no less than thirty-four lines to complete this sentence.[14] Apart from the fact that it is unbecoming in him, as the ruler of Milan, to indulge in such levity, it shows bad manners and a cynical, satirical temperament. It has been pointed out that his wit is of a negative kind: "It is cynical and cruel."[15]

He had treacherously deposed his own brother in the not-so-distant past, and deliberately set him and Miranda afloat to perish. The intervening twelve years have not brought about any improvements in his nature. At his very first appearance we had seen him as a most unprepossessing character and, on the island, at the first opportunity, he tries to make Sebastian betray Alonso and kill him. He tempts the unwary Sebastian:

> And yet methinks I see it in thy face,
> What thou shouldst be. Th' occasion speaks thee, and
> My strong imagination sees a crown
> Dropping upon thy head.[16]

His eloquence persuades Sebastian, though the latter is at first unwilling or perhaps unable to believe that he can become the King of Naples. Sebastian remembers that Antonio had come by his own dukedom by betrayal and asks him if his conscience does not trouble him. Antonio does not have any vestiges of a conscience:

> Ay, sir, where lies that? If't were a kibe
> 'Twould put me to my sleeper, but I feel not
> This deity in my bosom. Twenty consciences
> That stood 'twixt me and Milan, candied be they,
> And melt ere they molest.[17]

This makes it abundantly clear that he has no sense of the sanctity of moral values, or of family relationships either. His is a heart of stone.

As soon as he has persuaded Sebastian to think along the lines he dictates, he wastes no time in implanting the thought of murder, and, as soon as this is done, he translates thought into action:

> Draw together,
> And when I rear my hand, do you the like
> To fall it on Gonzalo.[18]

This change from idle fooling to successful plotting has been praised by E.M.W. Tillyard:

> Antonio's transformation from the cynical and lazy badgerer of Gonzalo's loquacity to the brilliantly swift and unscrupulous man of action is a thrilling affair.[19]

Antonio has been compared, in this respect, with Iago in *Othello* who also presents a similar facet of his character. The difference between the two lies chiefly in the fact that though there is a motive behind Antonio's plotting (exemption from paying tribute to the King of Naples), there is none in what Coleridge has called the "motiveless malignity" of Iago.

The two of them are prevented from executing their plan and Antonio, with great presence of mind, talks about a terrible noise to account for the fact that both of them had drawn swords in their hands.

We see him next in the feast-scene. It is most significant that here, after Ariel's diatribe, he is not truly repentant as Alonso is. He is taken aback at first, and Sebastian reacts before he does.

Sebastian : But one fiend at a time
I'll fight their legions o'er.

Antonio : I'll be thy second.[20]

Sebastian takes it for granted that Ariel and the other spirits are all evil ones who have come to frighten them. He is prepared to fight them and Antonio agrees with him. He is terrified at present but not penitent. Later, spellbound by Prospero's magic, all these characters reach the threshold of madness, but after being released from the spell Antonio remains the same—unscrupulous and evil. Prospero has insight into everyone's mind and says:

You, brother mine, that entertain'd ambition,
Expell'd remorse and nature.[21]

It is remarkable that even after being released from the spell he does not say anything, not even when, of his free will and unasked, Prospero forgives him. As a matter of fact he has not been given any lines in the long last scene. Everyone speaks, but not he. Instead, he recedes into the background. Shakespeare knew that there are certain types of men who are so totally evil that they cannot be reformed. If they did, it would be a destruction of their personality itself. He, therefore, accepts the presence of evil and does not introduce a change in Antonio which would have gone against his nature and also violated the fourth rule given by Aristotle, the rule of consistency. A change into a penitent would not have been consistent with the character of Antonio. The feature has been noticed by R.A. Andretta, though he does not connect it with Aristotle.

> Shakespeare therefore shows his usual deep insight into human nature by not making this unregenerate Machiavellian character change or express any sorrow when Prospero faces him at the end and offers him forgiveness.[22]

Antonio thus remains, to the very end, unrepentant and unreformed. Prospero realises this fact and, therefore, though he forgives him, yet keeps him in his power. He tells both him and Sebastian that he keeps the information that they had planned to kill Alonso for possible future use:

> Were I so minded
> I here could pluck his highness's frown upon you
> And justify you traitors. At this time
> I will tell no tales.[23]

This is perfectly understandable. It is just as well that persons like Antonio should have something, or someone, to curb them.

(d) Sebastian

Sebastian, the brother of Alonso, makes up the pair of entirely negative characters in the play when coupled with Antonio. The evil in his nature is dormant and becomes active when instigated by Antonio. It is Antonio who awakens his ambition. His fault is that he is too malleable, like a mass of clay in Antonio's hands, to be shaped as Antonio wants. He acquiesces in everything that Antonio says:

> Prithee, say on.
> The setting of thine eye and cheek proclaims
> A matter from thee.[24]

As soon as Antonio tells him to accept the fact that Ferdinand is dead, Sebastian agrees. Then when Antonio says that Claribel (who, next to Ferdinand, is the heir) is married and too far off to create any trouble, Sebastian agrees with this as well. Next when Antonio tells him that now, while everyone is asleep, is the best time to kill Gonzalo as well as Alonso, he agrees:

> Thy case, dear friend,
> Shall be my precedent: As thou got'st Milan,

I'll come by Naples. Draw thy sword—one stroke
Shall free thee from the tribute which thou payest,
And I the king shall love thee.[25]

He reveals himself, thus, as a weak character, too easily led. Yet this has become possible because there is evil in his nature. When in the feast-scene Antonio is not able to react and stands still as if turned to stone, Sebastian shows him the way by saying that he is ready to fight the devils of the island. The evil within him makes him see evil around him. Like Antonio he finds the island to be barren and inhospitable and this reveals the inner core of evil in him.

He, like Antonio, remains unrepentant to the end. Prospero, in the long speech he delivers before he sets these men free, refers to him.

Thy brother was a furtherer in the act—
Thou art pinch'd for't now, Sebastian...
Whose inward pinches therefore are most strong.[26]

This refers to Sebastian's mental anguish, but it is not supported by his speech or action. He speaks very little in the last scene. Moreover, Prospero seems to recognise that, like Antonio, his nature is so steeped in evil that nothing can reform it. He, therefore, holds the secret of his plot against Alonso over his head as a threat. This will enable Prospero to control him in case of future devilry.

(e) Adrian

Just as Antonio and Sebastian make up a pair of negative characters, so do Adrian and Francisco make up the pair of positive characters. Like Gonzalo, Adrian too finds the island a very pleasant place. He is hardly allowed to speak by Antonio and Sebastian. They interrupt him three times in one sentence, but without losing his temper he affirms that though the island is apparently inhospitable, it is not actually so:

It must needs be of subtle, tender
and delicate temperance.... The air
breathes upon us here most sweetly.[27]

He does not speak much after this, except to exclaim at Antonio's witticism "widow Dido." After this he does not speak at all, yet it can definitely be said that, within the few lines that have been given to him he comes alive as a positive character, supporting Gonzalo in his view of the island.

(f) Francisco

This character, like Adrian, is a part of Alonso's retinue and speaks but twice in the play. He too, like Adrian, is a positive character. Moreover, he consoles Alonso by telling him that Ferdinand may be alive for he had seen him swimming towards the shore:

> Sir, he may live.
> I saw him beat the surges under him.
> . . . . I do not doubt
> He came alive to land.[28]

This speech, ten lines long, is quite a lengthy one for a minor character and serves the purpose of an attempt at consoling Alonso who, however, remains disconsolate. After this he speaks only half a line in the feast-scene, voicing the wonder felt by all of them. Characters like Adrian and Francisco serve the important purpose of providing a background against which the main characters play their part. They prove the existence of a society made of ordinary human beings leading ordinary lives against which the main characters are highlighted.

(g) Trinculo

Trinculo, designated as Alonso's jester, is the first of the comic characters to enter the stage. He along with Stephano and Caliban, has been put into the group of comic characters which, according to G.W. Knight, constitutes the third group of characters in this play. Trinculo is the court jester and at once reminds us of Shakespeare's famous jesters like Touchstone, Feste and Lear's Fool. He is, however, a Fool of a very different kind, being a Fool of a very inferior status. He has little wit and no keenness of intellect:

> *The Tempest* is an austere work. The poet, while giving his clowns full rein in comic appeal, allows them no dignity.[29]

So Trinculo is so frightened at the approach of a storm that he creeps under Caliban's cloak, and this in spite of the fact that he perceives Caliban to be a monster.

Besides providing comic relief Trinculo also serves another important purpose—he is the only character who gives a description of Caliban, however fragmentary it might be:

> A fish, he smells like a fish,
> a very ancient and fish like smell; A kind of
> not-of-the-newest poor-John.... Legged
> Like a man and his fins like arms![30]

There is very little description of Caliban as it is, and this is the longest. He also gives us his opinion of Caliban's mental capacities:

> ...this is a very shallow monster.
> I afeard of him? A very weak monster....
> A most poor, credulous monster.[31]

As Caliban makes much of Stephano, Trinculo goes on commenting upon Caliban ("a howling monster; a drunken monster!"). Later, all three of them, gloriously drunk, plot Prospero's murder, and then go out, following Ariel's invisible music. In this entire scene Trinculo shows himself as a man who takes the lead offered by Stephano. They fall into the bog and get besmirched in its filthy waters. When they see the robes hung out for them, he reaches out for one but as soon as Stephano wants it, gives it up. He has already accepted Stephano as the would-be king of the island.

It is true that as a Fool Trinculo comes nowhere near the famous Fools of Shakespeare, but he does provide comic laughter in the play.

(h) Stephano

Stephano is the last of the characters to come on the stage. He has been designated as Alonso's butler, and in the last scene Alonso recognises him as such:

> Is not this Stephano, my drunken butler?[32]

Indeed, we never see him sober on the stage. When he enters, in the second scene of the second Act, he is already drunk. He had escaped drowning by clinging to a butt of sack and is now making full use of that wine. He is already half-drunk by the time that he meets Trinculo, and cannot bear to be turned around for fear of throwing up the wine. It is on account of the wine that he provides that he gains Caliban's admiration and allegiance. He accepts this devotion and soon enough starts fancying himself as the king of the island, with Miranda as the prospective queen:

> Monster, I will kill this man. His
> daughter and I will be king and queen
> —save our graces—and Trinculo and
> thyself shall be viceroys.[33]

All this courage, however, is just pot-valour, for he gets frightened by the music Ariel produces.

Later when they are drenched in filthy water he behaves right royally, bestowing garments upon Trinculo for having pleased him with a jest.

> I thank thee for that jest: here's a
> garment for't
> ...Wit shall not go unrewarded while I am King of this
> country.[34]

He is a drunken clown and comparing him with Falstaff and Sir Toby Belch, G. Wilson Knight finds him to be totally inferior. His desire to be the king of the island is compared by Wilson Knight with the hunger for power as found in Tamburlaine.

> He becomes a petty tyrant and engages in a bloody plot, aiming to make himself the lord of the island. He is a burlesque of the power quest.[35]

As a matter of fact Stephano is too light and low a character to be taken so seriously. He is but a clown and should not be compared seriously with great tragic figures like Tamburlaine or Macbeth.

There is one aspect of his character which has to be mentioned: he has an off-hand good-natured kindness for Caliban. He finds Caliban trembling with fear when he sees him for the first time. He takes this trembling to be the signs of an ague, and gives him the best remedy that he can think of—a draught of wine. Trinculo talks of beating Caliban but Stephano always treats him with kindness. This good-humoured kindness to one who is but a monster should be remembered as a positive quality of his character.

(i) The Master of the Ship

The Ship-Master is the first to enter the stage and speak. He comes for a very short time and speaks very little, but within this short time he leaves the impression of being an efficient and energetic captain. After this he comes on the stage only in the last scene and there, too, he does not speak. He enters along with the Boatswain and one would think that it is for him to reassure Alonso about the well-being of the ship and her crew. Gonzalo, however, overlooks him and speaks to the Boatswain, and therefore the Ship-Master keeps quiet, showing proper deference to his betters.

(j) The Boatswain (Bosun)

The Boatswain is the second character to enter the stage. He is a loquacious man and is also a man who is rather impatient by nature. He shows no deference to the royal party if they interfere in his work. Death is staring them in the face and the aristocrats are merely hindering his work when they come out on the deck:

> You mar our labours. Keep your
> cabins—you do assist the storm.[36]

He becomes even more outspoken when Gonzalo tells him to be polite:

> You are a councillor; if you can command
> these elements to silence, and work
> the peace of the present, we will not hand
> a rope more—use your authority.[37]

This impatience with ineffective courtiers does not spell disrespect, it is only the pardonable impatience of an efficient man when life itself is in danger. Gonzalo understands it as such and takes heart from it, thus proving his own sensibleness.

The Bosun comes again in the last scene and it is to him that Gonzalo speaks. Now that all danger is past he speaks with due deference, in blank verse, whereas he had spoken in prose before. He reassures everyone about the ship's safety:

> The best news is that we have safely found
> Our king and company; the next, our ship,
> Which but three glasses since we gave out split,
> Is tight and yare and bravely rigg'd as when
> We first put out to sea.[38]

After this, when ordered by Alonso to recount what had happened to them, he speaks a passage in verse, recounting how they had been put to sleep and finally brought to the cave. The poet has given more lines to him than to the captain and he stands out as a rounded-out individual character.

* * *

All the main as well as the minor characters can thus be seen to be thoroughly realistic individuals, for, however, short a time they might come on the stage. Our poet gives them a personality even if they speak but one line. The Bosun is the most remarkable of these. As a matter of fact, the first scene is doubly effective because of this man. Analysing the first scene, Coleridge has observed:

> Shakespeare had predetermined to make the plot of this play such as to involve a certain number of low characters and at the same time he pitched the note of the whole.[39]

REFERENCES

1. Act I, sc. ii, *ll.* 161-64, p. 11.
2. Act II, sc. i, *ll.* 164-65, p. 33.
3. Kermode, F., *Introduction to The Tempest*, in Palmer, *op. cit.*, p. 179.
4. Knight, G.W., *op. cit.*, p. 141.
5. Act III, sc. iii, *ll.* 31-34, p. 59.
6. Act V, sc. i, *ll.* 201-04, p. 83.
7. Act V, sc. i, *ll.* 118-19, p. 79
8. Act V, sc. i, *ll.* 197-98, p. 83.
9. Act II, sc. i, *ll.* 125-28, p. 32.
10. Knight, G.W., *op. cit.*, p. 141.

11. Act II, sc. i, *ll.* 103-04, p. 31.
12. Cutts, J.P., *Music and the Supernatural in The Tempest*, in Palmer, *op. cit.*, p. 203.
13. Act I, sc. i, *ll.* 42, p. 2.
14. Act II, sc. i, *ll.* 15-49. pp. 27-29.
15. Knight, G.W., *op. cit.*, p. 142.
16. Act II, sc. i, *ll.* 203-06, pp. 35-36.
17. Act II, sc. i, *ll.* 273-77, p. 38.
18. Act II, sc. i, *ll.* 291-93, p. 39.
19. Tillyard, E.M.W., *op. cit.*, p. 124.
20. Act III, sc. iii, *ll.* 102-03, p. 62.
21. Act V, sc. i, *ll.* 75-76, p. 78.
22. Andretta, R.A., *op. cit.*, p. 84.
23. Act V, sc. i, *ll.* 126-28, p. 80.
24. Act II, sc. i, *ll.* 225-27, p. 36.
25. Act II, sc. i, *ll.* 287-91, p. 39.
26. Act V, sc. i, *ll.* 73-77, p. 78.
27. Act II, sc. i, *ll.* 42-46, pp. 28-29.
28. Act II, sc. i, *ll.* 110-19, p. 31.
29. Knight, G. Wilson, *op. cit.*, p. 145.
30. Act II, sc. ii, *ll.* 25-33, pp. 41-42.
31. Act II, sc. ii, *ll.* 141-43, p. 45.
32. Act V, sc. i, 277, p. 86.
33. Act III, sc. ii, *ll.* 104-06, p. 56.
34. Act IV, sc. i, *ll.* 240-42, p. 73.
35. Knight, G. Wilson, *op. cit.*, p. 146.
36. Act I, sc. i, *ll.* 13-14, p. 1.
37. Act I, sc. i, *ll.* 19-22, p. 2.
38. Act V, sc. i, *ll.* 221-25, p. 84.
39. Coleridge, *op. cit.*, p. 51.

9

The Plot-Structure or Dramatic Strategies

There are certain features that all plays have in common and plot, which Aristotle calls "the soul of tragedy", is one of them. One basic difference that leaps to the eye as far as comedies are concerned is that, whereas tragedies have an unhappy end, comedies end happily. In addition, comedies usually have a more complex structure than tragedies, for they have more intrigues and episodes than tragedies have. The rules governing the structure of plays have been handed down by classical theorists, at whose head stands Aristotle, and these rules were well-known by Shakespeare and the other dramatists of his age. The rules that Aristotle had laid down for tragedies are, in general, held to be applicable to all drama, though there are some that are specifically meant for tragedies. Some such basic rules will now be mentioned.

The Rules of the Unities

The so-called rules of the three unities—unity of time, place and action, generally atributed to Aristotle, came to England mainly through the writings of the critics of the Italian Renaissance: Scaliger, Mintrerno, Castelvestro and others. However, these rules have become famous under the name of the Three Unities. These are: (a) the Unity of Action, (b) the Unity of Time and (c) the Unity of Place. It is a well-known fact that Shakespeare did not take these rules very seriously, but there are always exceptions, and *The Tempest* is one such exception. This is the only play of Shakespeare in which he has not only consciously observed the rules, but has repeatedly called attention to this fact as Ben Jonson does.

(a) **The Unity of Action.** This rule implies that there should be no mingling of serious and trivial actions. This rule is specially important for tragedies, but is relevant for comedies as well. A comedy should not have serious and tragic actions or scenes just as a tragedy should not have comic actions in it. Pity and terror, which are the emotions produced by tragic actions, are the emotions that have been relegated to tragedies. Comedies should have actions that produce laughter. The rule is more relevant for satirical comedies but it applies to romantic ones as well.

This becomes clear when we consider the fact that in Shakespeare's comedies we often come across serious actions as well as comic ones. Even the serious actions, however, are not productive of pity and terror except in the case of Shylock in *The Merchant of Venice*. In the play under discussion, for example, no less than two murders are planned. None, however, is executed. Both are foiled almost as soon as planned. The shipwreck in the first scene produces both pity and terror, but these emotions are dispelled very soon; they do not linger. They occur at the very outset and the reader is soon assured that everyone is safe. The shipwreck, moreover, is in the nature of a prologue, and is over before the actual action starts.

(b) **The Unity of Time.** Ideally, the time covered by the play should be as much as is covered by the actual performance on the stage. If the performance time is two hours, then the action of the play should also cover two hours. This seems to be quite impossible, but the classical dramatists had achieved this ideal. Aristotle, however, was very liberal in his views and he had allowed "a single revolution of the sun". The story of a play should take about a full day. This, too, is quite difficult, but not impossible. Ben Jonson, for example, takes no more than a full day for his plays, from early morning till evening.

Shakespeare, as has been said before, does not care much about the rules. In the Chronicle plays, for example, it is not possible to observe this rule at all, since such plays, of necessity, have to cover a long span of time. In his other plays also he does not care about this rule. The most widely known violation of this rule occurs in one of the last romances itself, *The Winter's Tale*, in which sixteen years are covered.

The case is otherwise with the play we are studying. Here the entire action takes just a few hours and Shakespeare calls attention to this feature repeatedly in the play. This feature is so important that it will be discussed in detail in the section entitled The Plot of *The Tempest.* It will be sufficient to note here that Shakespeare, if and when so needed, could observe the classical rules as strictly as any scrupulous classical scholar.

(c) The Unity of Place. According to this rule, there should be no changes of scenes in a play. The action should take place in one place only. This is nearly impossible, though the classical dramatists had managed to do it. Among the Elizabethans, Ben Jonson has faithfully observed the rule, though he gives a few changes of scenes.

Shakespeare, it has to be pointed out again, did not observe this rule either. His plays range not only to different places in the same city or country, but even over different kingdoms. The neo-classical critics of his own time and of later times, had condemned him. One of the greatest Neo-classical critics, Dr. Johnson, however, had defended him.

Once more it needs to be pointed out that *The Tempest* is an exceptional play in this respect. Here Shakespeare has observed all the classical rules, including the rule of the unity of place. The entire play takes place within the periphery of a small island, though there are some changes of scene within this island.

These and many other rules about plot were laid down by Aristotle. His rules were later commented upon and explained by other scholars. Aristotle was not so easily available to the Elizabethans as the Latin works were. The works of Horace, Quintilian, and others were studied more in detail by them. One such critic was Donatus. He has explained Aristotle's theories in detail and also added his own explanations. According to him the first section of the play is the Prologue.

This is usually a short speech occurring before the actual action of the play begins. It tells the reader about the theme and the story of the play itself. Marlowe's Prologue to *Dr. Faustus* is a very good example of a prologue written in the classical manner. Shakespeare, too, has written prologues to a few of his plays. Usually he incorporates them within the first scene of the play, as is the case with *The Tempest*. There are three plays where there are separate prologues—*Romeo and Juliet, Troilus and Cressida* and *Henry VIII*. Three others have speeches given by the Chorus or some other characters before the action starts; but they are not called prologues—*Henry IV Pt. II, Henry V* and *Pericles*. *The Tempest* does not have a prologue as such. Instead it has the highly dynamic storm-scene which precedes the main action of the play.

Besides these there are certain other rules for drama that were known and practised by the Elizabethan dramatists, in tragedy as well as in comedy. "Peripeteia" or the Reversal of fortune is such a device. It is usually employed to the hero of a tragedy and as such has a negative sense, because it implies the fall of the hero from a high into a low status. When used with reference to comedy, however, it has a positive sense for it will mean a change from adversity to prosperity or from misery to bliss. When we see Ferdinand he has lost everything and is stranded on an island without any means of escape. Things become, as he thinks, even worse, for he becomes a slave. Then his state improves, he gets everything that he had, that is, the father he had thought to be dead, the heirdom of Naples. More than anything else, he gets Miranda.

Very much the same is the case with the other characters as well. All of the shipwrecked party lose everything and then a time of happiness ensues for each of them.

Prospero's case is highly ambiguous. It is true that he loses the lordship of a wild island and goes to gain his dukedom back. From this point of view it is a change from adversity to prosperity. Yet it must be remembered that what he renounces is a truly great power—a power that men may dream of but never get. Not only does he have power over the world of nature, but over men also. He says in the renunciation speech:

I have bedimm'd
The noontide sun, call'd forth the mutinous winds,
And 'twixt the green sea and the azur'd vault
Set roaring war; to the dread rattling thunder
Have I given fire, and rifted Jove's stout oak
With his own bolt.[1]

Besides this power over the world of nature he has power over man's body as well as his mind. He stills Ferdinand with but a wave of his wand so that Ferdinand cannot move, and later he casts such a spell over Alonso and his party that they are bemused and confused to such an extent that they are in a half-conscious state. Ariel makes their pitiable state clear in a moving speech:

They cannot budge till your release. The king,
His brother, and yours, abide all three distracted,
And the remainder mourning over them
. . . . your charm so strongly works 'em
That if you now beheld them, your affections
Would become tender.[2]

This is the peak of man's worldly power—to have full control over Nature and Man. From this point of view the mere dukedom of a state would look paltry. Yet Prospero chooses the latter. His case, therefore, defies the conventional understanding of Peripeteia.

Another important element of the plot is Recognition or Anagnorisis. This, at its simplest, means the mutual recognition of characters who, for some reason, have been separated from each other. The Recognition-scene in *Twelfth Night* is Recognition of this kind. The subtlest kind of recognition is self-recognition, when a character recognises the quirks of his own personality.

There are different kinds of recognition in this play. The most superficial kind of recognition, *i.e.*, the recognition of individuals who have been separated, occurs twice in the last Act. First comes the recognition of Prospero by the ship's party. He announces himself to the others thus:

Behold, sir king,
The wronged duke of Milan, Prospero.[3]

Alonso, full of wonder, recognizes him, though he still cannot believe that it is really Prospero and not any apparition, even after being embraced by him:

Whe'er thou beest he or no
Or some enchanted trifle to abuse me,
As late I have been, I not know.[4]

The second instance of recognition is a markedly trivial one. Stephano and Trinculo, besmirched with mud, wearing cheap finery over their dirty bodies, and drunk, are recognised by Alonso and Sebastian:

Alonso : Is not this Stephano, my drunken butler?
Seb. : He is drunk now—where had he wine?
Alon. : And Trinculo is reeling-ripe.[5]

These are fairly ordinary examples of recognition. A much more subtle one occurs when Caliban recognises his own foolishness on seeing real kings:

I'll be wise hereafter,
And seek for grace. What a thrice-double ass
Was I to take this drunkard for a god,
And worship this dull fool![6]

This is true self-recognition, not very easy to come across in plays.

Very often, specially in comedies, the plot becomes so intricate that it becomes difficult to bring about a happy ending. In such cases there is the classical strategy of the *deus ex machina*. In the classical plays a god, like Apollo, Zeus, etc., would come on the stage and smooth out all the difficulties so that a happy ending can be brought about. In English plays this function is relegated to some person of authority like the king, the duke, etc. Aristotle is not in favour of this device, but it has been widely used by dramatists. In this play Prospero has been regarded as a *deus ex machina*:

> The fundamental perspective is provided by Prospero as a *deus ex machina* figure.[7]

This, indeed, is a well-recognised fact. Prospero does control the entire action and this fact has been pointed out by various critics. Prospero, like a puppet-master, controls everyone, spirits and humans alike, and he does so through his magic, which some critics call his art. Both Frank Kermode and Rose Zimbardo use the word "art" instead of "magic":

> Prospero is an artist who controls through his art. There is no suspense in the play because Prospero can control future as well as present action.[8]

This is far more serious than the function of a *deus ex machina*. Shakespeare has taken Prospero well beyond the limits of such a figure.

Certain Elizabethan Features in *The Tempest*

Aristotle was not in favour of more than one plot in a play, and, indeed, in the Old Classical Comedy there is but one plot. As the New Classical Comedy developed, however, changes crept in and, in them very often there are two plots. The Elizabethans developed their plays after the model of this later comedy, as found mainly in Plautus and in Terence. Ben Jonson, following mainly Terence, made all his plays double-plotted at least, if not multiple-plotted. Shakespeare's plays also have more than one plot. Usually there is one main plot and one or more sub-plots in his plays. The sub-plots are usually comic ones, provoking laughter. *The Tempest* is a play with two plots—the main plot concerned with the noble characters and the sub-plot with the comic ones. There are also many intrigues.

In the main plot we see Prospero the deposed duke of Milan planning a secure future for his daughter and setting things in motion. His enemies, Alonso the King of Naples and Antonio his brother, are by chance sailing across the seas raised by magical arts so that their ship is wrecked. They themselves are unharmed and reach Prospero's island in safety. Alonso's son, the future king of Naples, is separated from the rest of the courtiers and the king and is brought to him. Ferdinand and Miranda fall in love and Prospero blesses their betrothal. Within this main plot there is an intrigue concerning the murder-plot hatched against Alonso by Antonio and Sebastian, but this is nullified by Prospero's vigilance.

The sub-plot is concerned with Trinculo, the court jester of Alonso, and Stephano his drunken butler in association with Caliban. They plot the murder of Prospero, but this too is foiled by him.

It is a point to be remembered that plots in the Elizabethan plays were not put together arbitrarily. There were definite schemes in the arrangements. For example, there is always some kind of relationship between the main and the sub-plots. In this play the relationship between the main and the sub-plots is one of parody. As L.S. Champion has pointed out:

> *The Tempest*, for the first time since *Twelfth Night*, provides a sub-plot which fully and extensively parodies the main.[9]

This element of parody is to be seen right from the very beginning. The most obvious example is the murder-plot. Just as Antonio and Sebastian plot the murder of Alonso, so do Trinculo, Sebastian and Caliban plot the murder of Prospero. Both are unsuccessful. Another example is the manner in which the characters are punished. Alonso, Antonio *et al.* are punished by Ariel in the feast-scene, after which Prospero casts a spell over them. Stephano and Trinculo fall into a ditch of filthy water and are pursued by spirits in the shape of dogs. Their punishment is not as heavy as in the case of the noble characters and provokes comic laughter whereas the punishment of the noble ones evokes serious thoughts and emotions.

The use of masques in plays is an Elizabethan custom that Shakespeare uses many times in his plays and the masque in *The Tempest* is one of the examples of his employment of this contemporary convention. It is a brief musical play-within-the-play, involving supernatural characters (as in this play), personification of different aspects of nature like seasons, etc. Masques can be very simple, as the one at the end of *Love's Labour's Lost*, which comprises just four songs sung by the four seasons, or elaborate mini-plays as the masque in this play.

The masque as a form of entertainment was very popular at Court and in the castles of noblemen and many masques were written by Ben Jonson for royal entertainment in which the courtiers themselves took part. The first of such masques, perfectly independent, was the *Masque of Blackness* by Ben Jonson in collaboration with Inigo Jones who designed the sets, in 1605. Thereafter, the masque became very popular as it provided music as well as spectacle, two of the elements of drama as given by Aristotle. As B. Blackstone remarks:

> It was a sort of embryonic opera treating of mythological and allegorical subjects, in which music, dance and elaborate decor existed on equal terms with poetry.[10]

It is a charming feature of the play that here the poet has made use of this colourful and highly appealing form of entertainment in order to celebrate the betrothal of Ferdinand and Miranda (*vide* Chapter 5, Scene-wise Analysis, *supra* and Chapter 11, Poetic Style, *infra*, for more details).

Adoption of disguises was a common procedure in Elizabethan plays. The most popular disguise in Shakespeare is the disguise of the heroine into a young man (Viola disguises herself as Cesario in *Twelfth Night* and Rosalind as Ganymede in *As You Like It*). This play does not have any such disguises. As a matter of fact no character in this play adopts any kind of disguise. Yet it has been suggested that disguise is present here in an indirect form. Prospero, as a magician, is said to be in disguise and he has to assume his rapier and hat as the Duke of Milan in order to be recognised by the others:

> Prospero's magic turns out to be a form of disguise: "Lie there, my art", and his magic powers are divested.[11]

This would mean that he is in disguise in almost the whole of the play as he appears without his robe only in part of the second scene. Whether this can be treated as a disguise is, however, a doubtful point (*vide* Chapter 10, Imagery and Symbolism, *Infra*).

The Sources of *The Tempest*

Most of the Elizabethan and Jacobean dramatists took the material for their plays from many different works which were already in existence. Old plays, narrative poems, romances, histories and other documents were used to provide the story of the play. As far as Shakespeare himself is concerned, the study of the sources from which he took his material has become an important branch of Shakespearean studies. It is most illuminating to see how he selects the material from half-a-dozen or more different sources, rejects some, retains some, elaborates some and concentrates some in accordance with his artistic requirements.

The Tempest is the only play of Shakespeare for which very little source material can be found. There are no plays or narrative poems from which he took the story. There are only a few contemporary non-fiction documents which can be said to have furnished some material for the play. These are:

(1) Three pamphlets describing the wreck of a fleet of nine ships on the Bermudas. These ships had been sent to strengthen the new colony in Virginia in 1609. The fleet met with a sudden storm and one particular ship, the Sea-Adventure, had perished with all its crew. The three pamphlets are:

(a) **A Discovery of the Bermudas** (1610), by Sylvester Jordan.

(b) **The True Declaration** of the state of the Colonie in Virginia with a confutation of such scandalous reports as have tended to the disgrace of so worthy an enterprise (1610), by the Council of Virginia.

(c) **True Repertory of the Wrack** (1610), by William Strachey.

(2) **The Essays of Michel de Montaigne** transl. by John Florio (1603).

(3) Ovid's **Metamorphoses**, transl. by Golding.

These sources have many pieces of information that Shakespeare used, there are many lines and phrases that have been echoed in *The Tempest*. What is most important, however, is that they do not provide the main story itself, which is entirely the poet's own:

> For once, Shakespeare had no objective story before him from which to create. He spins his plot from his own poetic world entirely.[12]

Out of the three pamphlets, Strachey has given an eye-witness account of the storm. It was a storm that lasted from Monday to Friday. There is one particular description which is very interesting:

> ...a little round light, like a faint star, trembled and streamed along with a sparkling blaze, half the height upon the main mast and shooting sometimes from shroud to shroud.[13]

This, known to the sailors as St. Elmo's Fire, is what Ariel describes when telling Prospero of his own feats:

> Sometimes I would divide
> And burn in many places; on the top-mast,
> The yards and the bowsprits would I flame distinctly,
> Then meet and join.[14]

Numerous echoes from this and the other pamphlets are to be found in the play. Strachey, for example, says that "the permissive providence of God" lay behind all the events, and Prospero, when asked by Miranda how they had reached the island, had replied "By providence divine."[15] No more explanation is offered, and, indeed, none is needed.

Two of Montaigne's essays are most significant in that one of them furnishes the basis for Gonzalo's utopia and the other for Prospero's idea of forgiveness. Thus, first of all, in the essay entitled *Of the Canniballes* Montaigne writes:

> It is a nation...that hath no kinde of trafficke, no knowledge of Letter, no intelligence of numbers, no name of magistrate, nor of politic superiority; no use of service, of riches, or of poverty; no contracts, no successions, no partitions, no occupation but idle.[16]

The essay goes on, describing more details, and many of these are repeated by Gonzalo:

> I' th' commonwealth, I would by contraries
> Execute all things, for no kind of traffic

Would I admit; no name of magistrate.
Letters should not be known, riches, poverty
And use of service none.[17]

Montaigne's essay, however, points out many negative aspects like quarrelling and fighting, having many wives, cannibalism, etc. Shakespeare omits all these negative details and presents Gonzalo's utopia as something that excels the golden age.

Medea, in Ovid's *Metamorphoses*, has a long speech that addresses the different aspects of the natural world and recounts her own magical exploits. This could have been the basis for Prospero's long renunciation-speech in the fifth Act.

Clearly, though Shakespeare took some of the ideas and phrases in his plays from the sources given above *The Tempest* remains the only play for which no proper dramatic or narrative sources can be found.

The Plot of *The Tempest*

The Tempest has two plots, with many intrigues in them: a serious main plot and a comic sub-plot. As has been pointed out above, the story is entirely his own, though he takes some details from certain sources. The story shows his individual and original talent for bringing together elements of romance (which the contemporary audience wanted) and those of farcical comedies (as handed down via the classical comedies). All this is mixed with the intrigues involving treachery and murder which give the play a serious overtone.

The main plot gives us the figure of Prospero the Duke of Milan who had been deposed twelve years ago and left to perish on the seas along with his daughter. They had reached an unnamed and uninhabited island. Though there are no human beings in the island now, it is inhabited by spirits. Prospero was a great magician and when he arrived he freed the spirit Ariel from a terrible imprisonment and established his supremacy over the entire island. All this now lies in the past, for when the play opens twelve years have passed since they landed and Miranda the daughter of Prospero is now a young lady of marriageable age.

Prospero's enemy, his brother Antonio, who had deposed him and left him to perish, and Alonso, the King of Naples who had helped Antonio, are passing by this island, along with Ferdinand the son of Alonso and other persons. Prospero knows of this and causes a storm in the sea by his magical powers. It is here that the real action begins. The ship is wrecked and all the characters reach the island. Ferdinand is separated from the rest of the royal party and is brought to Prospero. Here he and Miranda see each other and fall deeply in love. This is exactly what Prospero had wanted, and, after testing the sincerity of Ferdinand's love, he blesses the two of them.

A murder-plot is hatched by Antonio and Sebastian to kill Alonso which is foiled by Prospero. Finally all the characters are re-united at the end of the play. Prospero forgives his enemies and decides to renounce his magical powers and go back to Milan as its Duke. The play ends happily for everyone.

The sub-plot is completely farcical. It involves two characters from Alonso's ship—Trinculo his jester, and Stephano his butler. Caliban, the monster offspring of the witch Sycorax, joins them in this comic sub-plot: He starts worshipping Stephano as a god and then instigates the two of them to kill Prospero. Stephano will then become the king of the island and marry Miranda.

The two plots, on the face of it, seem to have nothing in common. The main plot has a romantic end in view—the union of Ferdinand and Miranda, but it also has the dark element of treachery and murder. Shakespeare has woven these two plots together with great artistry, as the scheme given below will make amply clear:

Act I—scene i	–	The storm at sea in which Alonso's ship perishes.
scene ii	–	Prospero tells Miranda of their previous history. Ferdinand and Miranda meet and fall in love.
Act II—scene i	–	Alonso's party reach the island. They think Ferdinand is dead. Antonio and

	Sebastian plot to kill Alonso but are prevented by Ariel.
scene ii –	Trinculo and Stephano reach the island and meet Caliban who takes Stephano for a god.
Act III—scene i –	Ferdinand and Miranda declare their love for each other.
scene ii –	Caliban, Stephano and Trinculo plot the murder of Prospero. Ariel reports this to Prospero.
scene iii –	Alonso's party reach a banquet spread by Prospero's spirits. Prospero remains on the stage, invisible to all. Ariel appears as a harpy and denounces the wrongdoers. Alonso is stricken by remorse.
Act IV –	Only one scene—Prospero, pleased with Ferdinand's genuine love for Miranda, blesses the two of them. A masque is presented to celebrate the betrothal. Caliban, Stephano and Trinculo reach the cave and are chased away by spirits in the shape of dogs.
Act V –	Only one scene—Prospero decides to renounce his magical powers and forgive his enemies. The royal party had been put under a spell which had made them powerless and nearly mad. They are restored to their senses and Prospero forgives them for the wrong they had done to him. Ferdinand is reunited to his father. All the crew of the ship are brought and it is learnt that the ship is safe. They will now leave the island for Naples.
The Epilogue –	Spoken by Prospero and tells how he will now spend his days as the Duke of Milan and not a mighty mage.

It can be seen from this scheme that Shakespeare is careful to alternate between the different groups of characters, usually presenting the main plot and the sub-plot in alternating scenes. Acts IV and V have only one scene each and in both of them the characters of both the plots are brought in:

> Much of the genius of Shakespeare is displayed in these happy combinations—the highest and the lowest, the gayest and the saddest.[18]

This mingling of the serious and the comic, however, should not be taken as a violation of the Aristotelian unity of action. As has been pointed out earlier in this chapter itself, Shakespeare has constructed this play with full regard for the rules of the three unities. It has to be remarked here that Shakespeare has not only observed these rules consciously, but, like Ben Jonson, has also drawn attention to the fact. Not only the unities, but certain other classical features are to be found in this play. Some of these have been discussed in the foregoing pages and some, which need more detailed discussion, will be mentioned now.

Shakespeare's five-Act structure accounts for and accommodates the progression of events as underlined by the classical rules. The play should, if traditional rules are followed, be preceded by a Prologue. *The Tempest* does not have a Prologue specifically designated as such. On the other hand the first scene is in the nature of a Prologue, as it takes place before the main action begins. Some, indeed, are of the opinion that the play has, not one Prologue, but two, for the first part of the second scene when Prospero recounts past history to Miranda, is very much like a Prologue:

> *The Tempest* possesses two prologues. The first of these is the dramatic one.... The other prologue consists of Prospero's account of how he had lost his dukedom and came to live on the uninhabited island.[19]

The action then begins, with Shakespeare rigidly conforming to the rules of the three unities. Unity of action has been observed in that tragic action does not occur in the play. It is true that there are two murder-plots in the play but both are foiled. No deaths take place. Since the play take place on one small island the unity of place has also been observed. More than any of these, it is the unity of time that repeatedly calls attention to itself. Shakespeare, in this respect, has outdone all his contemporaries, including even Ben Jonson. No less than four times does he call attention to the time. In the first Act Prospero asks and Ariel answers:

> Pros. : What is the time o' th' day?
>
> Ariel : Past the mid-season.
>
> Pros. : At least two glasses. The time 'twixt six and now
> Must by us both be spent most preciously.[20]

That is to say, the action will take place within four hours. Again in the third Act Prospero refers to the time.

> For yet ere suppertime must I perform
> Much business appertaining.[21]

Shakespeare reminds us that supper-time has not yet come, though it is not clear what o'clock it actually is. Then again in the last Act Prospero asks Ariel:

> Prospero : How's the day?
>
> Ariel : On the sixth hour, at which time, my lord
> You said our work should cease.[22]

The next reference to time is made by Bosun, who says:

> Our ship,
> Which but three glasses since we gave out split
> Is tight and yare and bravely rigg'd.[23]

The actual time covered by the action, thus, is about four hours. This is a miraculous achievement. Even Ben Jonson takes an entire day for his plays. It is only in the classical plays that a like instance can be found:

> It is a fact impossible to ignore that Shakespeare deliberately constructed the play in accordance with neo-Terentian rules.[24]

The plot of *The Tempest* has been interpreted in many different ways. E.M.W. Tillyard thinks that Shakespeare has crammed three plays into one. He lays stress on "the tragic pattern" in the play. There is the tragedy concerning Prospero's downfall twelve years ago. This is the tragedy of the past. After this there is the tragedy of the present, *i.e.,* the storm-scene and the two murder-plots. Then comes the theme of regeneration presented through Ferdinand and Miranda. According to him all these three aspects of the plot have been brought together in a masterly manner. The play is actually a compressed trilogy.

The Supernatural Element

Supernatural characters and events play a very important part in this play. The presence of such element, the element of "the marvellous" was recognised and appreciated by Aristotle:

> The marvellous should be represented in tragedy.... The marvellous is a source of pleasure.[25]

Though this remark refers specially to tragedy, it is applicable to all kinds of play. Aristotle had another famous remark to make in this connection:

> Probable impossibilities are to be preferred to improbable possibilities.[26]

Later critics, following these two guidelines, have developed their theories of the supernatural.

The element of the marvellous is present in our play from the very beginning to the end. As a matter of fact it permeates the entire play. The tempest itself is brought about by the magic of Prospero and the work of Ariel who is a supernatural creature; and, at the end, though Prospero has renounced his powers, yet he looks forward to being conveyed safely to Naples by Ariel's powers. It is a feature that cannot be overlooked and has been noticed by the early critics as well as more recent ones:

> He has there given the reins to his boundless imagination and has carried the romantic, the wonderful and the wild, to the most pleasing extravagance.[27]

The element of the supernatural is given here in many different ways. It is presented in the form of characters, as in

Ariel and the other spirits who repeatedly appear in the play—in the feast-scene and in the masque as the goddesses Juno, Iris and Ceres and the nymphs and the harvesters, and as the dogs chasing Stephano, etc. in the same scene. Apart from being presented in characters, the supernatural is also presented in the events that crowd into the play, for example the storm that causes the shipwreck, the feast-scene, the masque, etc. Prospero's own supernatural powers are also used on human characters, as for example in the paralysing of Ferdinand in the second scene of the first Act, and the distraction amounting to madness induced in the royal party. Analysing this last element it can be said that there are two ways in which Prospero's magic is seen working in the play. First of all his power is the power of virtuous and holy magic as opposed to the evil magic of the witch Sycorax. This has given him power over nature as well as supernatural beings like Ariel and others. The most important function of his magic, however, is a symbolic one, for it has given him control over all passions. This is a valuable point made by F. Kermode:

> As a mage he controls nature, as a prince he conquers the passions which had excluded him from his own kingdom.[28]

The presence of the supernatural element is thus not only to give pleasure, as Aristotle had said, but it has many other functions as well. Prospero's power as a benevolent mage has given the island the unique quality of resounding with heavenly music and music stands for peace and harmony. Again, the supernatural feast spread for the royal party by supernatural agents has been compared with the feast given by Circe to her victims. The difference lies in the fact that Circe's feast turned men into animals, whereas Prospero's feast brings the stubborn and guilty men to a recognition of their guilt.

Magic and supernatural creatures in this play, as in *A Midsummer Night's Dream*, bring about harmony and unite those who have been separated. It gives not merely the dimension of the fantastic, but is highly functional as well.

REFERENCES

1. Act V, sc. i, *ll.* 41-46, p. 77.
2. Act V, sc. i, *ll.* 11-19, p. 76.
3. Act V, sc. i, *ll.* 106-07, p. 79.
4. Act V, sc. i, *ll.* 111-13, p. 79.
5. Act V, sc. i, *ll.* 277-79, p. 86.
6. Act V, sc. i, *ll.* 294-96, p. 86.
7. Champion, L.S., *op. cit,* p. 175.
8. Zimbardo, R.A., *Form and Disorder in The Tempest*, in Palmer, *op. cit.*, p. 236.
9. Champion, L.S., *op. cit.*, p. 183.
10. Blackstone, Bernard, *Shakespeare: The Tempest*, Notes on Literature series, Feb. 1969, issued by the British Council, London, 1969, p. 7.
11. Bradbrook, M.C., *op. cit.*, p. 205.
12. Knight, G. Wilson, *op. cit.*, p. 131.
13. The text, p. 90.
14. Act I, sc. ii, *ll.* 198-201, p. 12.
15. Act I, sc. ii, line 169, p. 11.
16. Quoted by Murry, J. Middleton, *op. cit.*, p. 115.
17. Act II, sc. i, *ll.* 144-48, p. 33.
18. Coleridge, *op. cit.*, p. 50.
19. Kott, Jan, *op. cit.*, p. 244.
20. Act I, sc. ii, *ll.* 239-41, p. 14.
21. Act III, sc. i, *ll.* 95-96, p. 52.
22. Act V, sc. i, *ll.* 3-5, pp. 76-77.
23. Act V, sc. i, *ll.* 232-34, p. 84.
24. Zimbardo, R.A., *op. cit.*, p. 234.
25. Dorsch, T.S., ed. & transl., *Classical Literary Criticism*, Penguin Books, 1975, p. 68.
26. *Ibid.*
27. Warton, J. in Palmer, *op. cit.*, p. 37.
28. Kermode, F., *op. cit.*, p. 187.

10

Imagery and Symbolism

Images and symbols are elements that serve not only to embellish poetry but to make it more intensely effective as well. This is an aspect of Shakespearean drama that has been emphasized by the critics of modern times, and has been studied extensively as well as intensively. The function of his imagery, the relationship between his imagery and the theme of the play, the development of his imagery from the first play to the last, have all been carefully studied and analysed. H. Fluchère has given a definition of imagery:

> Imagery may shortly be defined as a concrete illustration drawn upon by the poet to clarify or embellish the object that he seeks to describe.[1]

Shakespeare's images, however, do not merely clarify or embellish, they have certain other dramatic functions as well.

The one basic fact that will have to be kept in mind while studying his imagery is that it is often impossible to differentiate between rhetorical figures, images and symbols. These three are integrally related and often there is an overlapping. That is, an image can be studied as a figure of speech and quite often it might be elevated into a symbol as well. This characteristic has been pointed out by H. Fluchère:

> No strict rule allows us to say at what point we pass from the plane of pure rhetoric, to the plane of pure psychology, and even the metaphysical plane, in the use of imagery.[2]

Moreover, according to the method of categorisation, the same image will come under different categories, *i.e.*, a sense image will also be a nature image or a domestic image or any other. This latter is a universal feature of images.

Sense-images are the most obvious and elementary kind of images. They are of five kinds, corresponding to our five senses. Visual images refer to the eye, auditory images to the ear, olfactory images to the sense of smell, gustatory images to taste and tactile images are those pertaining to the sense of touch. There is another phenomenon related to sense-images, known as synaesthesia in which different sense-images mix and mingle.

Let us now look at some of the images to be found in only one scene, the second scene of the first Act. Shakespeare's poetry is extremely rich in sense-images. Ariel's famous description of how he appeared like a flame in many places at once is a very fine example of visual imagery:

> Sometimes I'd divide
> And burn in many places; on the topmast,
> The yard and the bowsprit would I flame distinctly
> Then meet and join.[3]

Visual images are quite common, but tactile ones are less so. There is a very effective tactile image in Ariel's description of Ferdinand's grief:

> Whom I left cooling of the air with sighs
> In an odd angle of the isle.[4]

This image is also remarkable because usually sighs are known to be hot, yet here Ferdinand is pictured as "cooling" the air with his sighs.

Apart from sense-images there are many other kinds of images, nature images being the most prominent among them. Shakespeare's wonderful ability to present nature images had been recognised by his early critics. Thus Dryden, who did not approve of the extra-ordinary world of Shakespearean imagery, could not help but praise his nature images:

> All the images of nature were still present to him and he drew them, not laboriously, but luckily; when he describes anything, you more than see it, you feel it too.[5]

Both of the images quoted above, in addition to being sense-images, are also nature images, for they describe fire and air respectively, which are two of the basic elements of nature. Besides these element-images there are animal and tree images as well. A very fine tree-image occurs quite early in the play. This is how Prospero describes his treacherous brother, in an effective and memorable way:

> That now he was
> The ivy which had hid my princely trunk,
> And suck'd my verdure out on't.[6]

Animal images are particularly effective and occur again and again. In order to emphasize the lack of sea-worthiness of the boat in which he and Miranda had been set adrift Prospero describes it as:

> A rotting carcass of a butt, not rigg'd
> Nor tackle, sail nor mast—the very rats
> Instinctively have quit it.[7]

This passage has one powerful animal image—that of the dead body of an animal. The fact that living rats instinctively left it reinforces the image by substantiating the point that the ship was virtueless.

The above passage, in addition, describes a boat, *i.e.*, it is a nautical image and there are many of them to be found here. The very opening speech by Miranda contains a nautical image describing the wrecked ship:

> a brave vessel—
> Who had, no doubt, some noble creature in her
> Dash'd all to pieces.[8]

Sea-images are so important in the play that they should be considered separately from other nature images. In fact the sea is present here throughout the play, not just in imagery, but as a symbol. Miranda's first description of the sea presents it in the turbulence of storm:

> The sky, it seems, would pour down stinking pitch,
> But that the sea, mounting to th' welkin's cheek
> Dashes the fire out.[9]

But the sea is not always like this, it can be calm and benevolent also. The most famous sea-image, occurring in Ariel's song "Full fathom five", presents the sea as a transforming agent, turning bones into corals and eyes into pearls. These images, moreover, also show Shakespeare's ability to take up a convention and use it for his own ends. What H. Fluchère calls "the laudatory image" is one of the most conventional kind of images. Eyes being compared with pearls and bones with coral are conventional laudatory images, but in our poet's hands they have become the agents of magnificent transformation. (For more details see the section on Symbolism, *infra.*)

There are many astronomical images scattered throughout the play. All the events of the play, starting from the storm itself, had been put initially in motion because of what the stars had foretold:

> I find my zenith doth depend upon
> A most auspicious star, whose influence
> If now I court not, but omit, my fortunes
> Will ever droop.[10]

Thus speaks Prospero and he does not take heed only of what the 'stars had foretold,' he knows that it is God who controls all events and as such there are many religious images. Thus in but half a line he voices his faith: "By providence divine."[11] This is a brief and abstract image, yet an extraordinarily effective one, for it echoes a religious faith that is universal and not merely Christian. A more concrete Christian image occurs in the same page when Prospero describes baby Miranda:

> O, a cherubim
> Thou wast that did preserve me.[12]

All these images are taken from only one scene of the play and besides these, there are many other images in the same scene well worth studying. This will serve to highlight the wealth of his imagery.

Analysing the imagery of *The Tempest*, W. Clemen points out several important features. It should be remembered that, according to him, just as Shakespeare's art developed and matured, so did his imagery. In the early plays we have images that serve to beautify the play, but as his art matured, gradually his imagery became more and more functional, integrally related to the play:

> The more Shakespeare becomes a conscious dramatic artist, the more he employs them for dramatic purposes. The images gradually lose their purely "poetic" often extraneous nature and become one of the dramatic elements.[13]

According to him images can anticipate events and can act proleptically thus imparting a sense of foreboding. There are many ways in which they also create the atmosphere of a scene or the entire play. There are several other functions of images as well. With reference to *The Tempest* he highlights the fact that here, instead of anticipating events or action, the imagery acts in a manner just the opposite. Most of the events have happened in the past, so the images serve to call back the past. Miranda describes the tempest she has seen and it recalls the turbulent sea which Prospero describes when the two of them were set adrift.

> There they hoist us,
> To cry to the sea that roar'd to us, to sigh
> To the winds.[14]

Clemen points out, among many other aspects, how in this play nature "does not stand for itself, but in some way continually affects human existence."[15] The nature images in the play, thus, are highly functional because they are related to human beings. The plants and the animals mentioned are described in terms of their effect on men. Many of these images portray nature as being hostile to man. Caliban on his firstly entry uses many nature images in cursing Prospero:

> As wicked dew as e'er my mother brush'd
> With raven's feather from unwholesome fen
> Drop on you both! a south-west blow on ye
> And blister you all o'er![16]

Prospero retaliates to this curse and uses a nature image which ordinarily has positive values, but in this case takes on highly negative associations:

Thou shall be pinch'd
As thick as honeycomb, each pinch more stinging
Than bees that made them.[17]

Honey and bees are traditionally associated with sweetness and light and are images which are highly positive, yet here they are used for a curse.

All these images are from only the second scene. It can be easily imagined what a wealth of imagery is to be found in the play if the whole of it is studied from this point of view. Let us now turn to the symbols in the play.

Symbolism

Many of Shakespeare's plays make use of symbols. It is not that he made conscious and deliberate use of symbolism but many of the features of his plays are so deeply fraught with meaning that they have attained the status of symbols. The last romances, specially, make extensive use of symbols. As a matter of fact, symbolism is usually recognised as a feature of romances:

> Romance results from welcoming the strange and especially from welcoming the symbols, perforce fantastic, in which foreign lands, and far away ages have sought to express their intimations of immortality.[18]

The Tempest, indeed, contains many important symbols and this is one of the factors that emphasize its essentially romantic nature (*Vide* Ch. 4, *supra*). The symbols of the play have been studied with care and a few of them will now be pointed out.

Music is definitely one of the most important symbols of this play. In his plays music often symbolises harmony. In *The Tempest* also it does the same. As such there is opposition between music and tempest, for just as music spells harmony so does tempest symbolise chaos and destruction. These two kinds of images are so significant that they cease to be mere images and are elevated to the status of symbols. As G. Wilson Knight has affirmed:

> The balance of tempest and music, not only in imagery but in plot too...here reaches its consummation.[19]

Music, as a matter of fact, pervades the entire play and the entire island. First of all there is invisible music, instrumental as well as vocal, often heard by Caliban:

> The isle is full of noises,
> Sounds, and sweet airs, that give delight, and hurt not.
> Sometimes a thousand twangling instruments
> Will hum about mine ears, and sometimes voices.[20]

Apart from this music which is, as it were, an essential feature of the island, there are the songs sung by Ariel. The first of these "Come unto these yellow sands", not only creates an atmosphere of beauty, love and harmony but also soothes Ferdinand's grief. The second song is of great importance in that it presents one of the key ideas of the play—transformation of mortal objects into objects of immortal beauty:

> Full fathom five thy father lies;
> Of his bones are coral made;
> Those are pearls that were his eyes,
> Nothing of him that doth fade,
> But doth suffer a sea-change
> Into something rich and strange.[21]

This wonderful song is symbolic of harmony as well as transformation. Moreover, as has been pointed out above, here Shakespeare takes up the conventional "Laudatory image" and gives it so much importance that it becomes symbolic.

After this, music as a symbol recurs again and again, reaching its climax in the masque. Juno and Ceres together sing a song which sums up all those ideas that make a marriage harmonious and peaceful. They bless the marriage of Ferdinand and Miranda with:

> Honour, riches, marriage-blessing
> Long continuance and increasing
> . . . .
> Earth's surcrease and foison plenty,
> Barns and garners never empty,
> Vines and clustering bunches growing
> Plants with goodly burden bowing [22]

From the very beginning to the end, music as a symbol of love and harmony gives not only great beauty but symbolic depth to the play. It is a thing that transforms grief into peace, mortality into immortal beauty and love into fruitful marriage. Ariel's last song shows music establishing a relationship between the physical world of nature and the ethereal nature of Ariel, and also establishes the continuance of this relationship even after Prospero has gone away. Summer after summer this relationship will continue.

Besides music there is the important symbol of the tempest. This, as opposed to music, symbolises disorder and destruction. The play is named after this symbol and the very first scene is a storm-scene. As Fluchère points out:

> Here everything is symbolic beginning with the title—the short title that is found in every play and is here merely a flashing prologue.[23]

In this scene we are shown how the elements of air and water are in a state of violent disorder that ends in destruction. Moreover, this storm has brought about disorder in the accepted social order as well, for the humble Bosun forgets his station and speaks rudely to royal persons. Later Prospero gives the description of high seas and howling winds when he was set adrift:

> There they hoist us
> To cry to the seas that roar'd to us, to sigh
> To th' winds.[24]

Ariel gives a long description of the tempest he raised in the sea, highlighting the feature of chaos and disorder. The very elements seem to have forsaken their essential nature for Ariel divides himself into several entities that appear like flames in many different places at the same time. Later again we see how this tempest has separated the crew and the passengers into separate groups.

It must be pointed out that though in his other plays a storm is usually the symbol of disorder and destruction yet here it is indirectly the cause of repentance, forgiveness and lover, and has a distant affinity with the storm in *King Lear*, which humanises Lear and gives him wisdom. As a matter of fact it is the cause of which the entire play is the effect. All the harm that the tempest has seemed to have done is, moreover, later seen to have been quite ineffectual, for the ship is made as good as new and everyone is safe.

Apart from these two important symbols there are many others in the play, Prospero's magic robe being one of them. This robe is symbolic of his magic power. He is already wearing it when he enters the stage and when he starts to recount their past history to Miranda he takes it off:

Lend thy hand
And pluck my magic garment from me.[25]

After he has told the story and Miranda has fallen asleep he puts on the cloak and it is only after that he calls Ariel. After this Shakespeare does not give any stage-directions about this robe till the last scene. It can, however, be surmised that perhaps he is wearing it when he, in the log-bearing scene, is invisibly present and looking at the courtship of Ferdinand and Miranda. Later in the masque scene he sets the spirit dogs at Trinculo and the others, while himself remaining invisible. Then in the last Act the stage-direction gives "Enter Prospero, in his magic robe". It is in this scene that the great abdication-speech occurs. Later, when the royal party is regaining their senses he says:

I will discase me, and myself present
As I was sometime Milan.[26]

The magic robe, thus, is symbolic of his powers and it also serves as a disguise (*Vide* Ch. 9, Plot, *supra*).

A rather minor symbol is the pool of dirty water into which the two comic characters fall. This pool is symbolic of their lack of moral cleanness as well as of their sensual nature.

Apart from having symbolic objects, this is a play in which the characters also invite symbolic interpretations. As has been pointed out, (*Vide,* Ch. 7, *supra*), Prospero is taken as a symbolic representation of the poet himself. Miranda has also been looked upon as a figure symbolising innocence and purity. These are aspects which she shares with Perdita, the heroine of *The Winter's Tale*. Likewise, Ariel and Caliban are also symbolic figures, Ariel symbolising the spirit of airy freedom and Caliban symbolising concrete earthiness.

The Tempest is thus a play exceptionally rich in imagery and symbolism. It is perhaps the only play of Shakespeare in which more characters are symbolic than any other.

REFERENCES

1. Fluchère, H., *op. cit.*, p. 167.
2. *Ibid.*, p. 167.
3. Act I, sc. ii, *ll.* 198-201, p. 12.
4. Act I, sc. ii, *ll.* 222-23, p. 14.
5. Enright, D.J. and Chickera, E.de, ed., *English Critical Texts: The Sixteenth Century to the Twentieth*, Oxford, The Univ. Press, 2002. Dryden, *An Essay on Dramatic Poesy, ll.* 1498-1500, p. 88.
6. Act I, sc. ii, *ll.* 85-87, pp. 7-8.
7. Act I, sc. ii, *ll.* 146-48, p. 10.
8. Act I, sc ii, *ll.* 6-9, p. 4.
9. Act I, sc. ii, *ll.* 3-5, p. 4.
10. Act I, sc.ii, *ll.* 181-84, p. 12.
11. Act I, sc. ii, *ll.* 159, p. 11.
12. Act I, sc. ii, *ll.* 152-53, p. 11.
13. Clemen, W., *The Development of Shakespeare's Imagery*, London, Methuen & Co. Ltd., 1977, p. 81.
14. Act I, sc. ii, *ll.* 148-50, p. 10.
15. Clemen, *op. cit.*, p. 189.
16. Act I, sc. ii, *ll.* 321-24, p. 18.
17. Act I, sc. ii, *ll.* 328-30, p. 18.
18. Whibley, Charles, ed., *George Wyndham : Essays in Romantic Literature*, N.Y., Books for Library Press, 1968, p. 36.
19. Knight, G. Wilson, *op. cit.*, pp. 131-32.
20. Act III, sc. ii, *ll.* 133-36, p. 57.
21. Act I, sc. ii, *ll.* 397-401, p. 21.
22. Act IV, sc. i, *ll.* 106-13, p. 68.
23. Fluchère, H., *op. cit.*, p. 266.
24. Act I, sc. ii, *ll.* 148-50, p. 10.
25. Act I, sc. ii, *ll.* 23-24, p. 5.
26. Act I, sc. i, *ll.* 85-86, p. 78.

11

Poetic Style: Diction and Versification

Shakespeare's poetic style is a very important aspect of his drama and has been studied at great length. There are many aspects of his style which, along with other elements, has served to make him the greatest English dramatist. His style reflects his age, that is, it is an Elizabethan-Jacobean style, and at the same time reflects his personality. Again the style is suited to each of the characters in the play. This is indeed a miracle.

It must be remembered that Shakespeare's plays, like all contemporary plays, were written in a mixture of prose and poetry. The noble characters (usually in the main plot) speak in verse and the humbler characters (usually in the sub-plot) speak prose. There are not many prose passages in our play and they shall be considered separately in this chapter. It should also be borne in mind that poetic style has two distinct divisions: diction and versification. These two aspects shall receive individual treatment.

(a) Poetic Diction

The classical theories of poetic diction were well-known in the Elizabethan times, particularly those of the Roman writers. Horace in his *Ars Poetica* had pointed out the rules of poetic diction. Not only should the diction vary according to the genre, but according to the character also. For example, the diction of elegies should be different from the diction of poems of love and in drama the characters should speak in a language that should be in conformity with their age, sex and social status:

> It will make a great difference whether a god or a hero is speaking, a man of ripe years or a hot-headed youngster in the pride of youth, a woman of standing or an officious nurse, a roving merchant or a prosperous farmer.[1]

This famous sentence has provided for differences in the speech of dramatic characters of all kinds. First of all, distinction is made between the divine and the human. Among human beings there are hundreds of varieties and poetic diction must be adjusted to all these. Age must be taken into account ("man of ripe years or a hot-headed youngster") and so must sex ("woman of standing"). Within these basic categories there are many sub-divisions according to age and social status, so Horace differentiated between a "woman of standing or an officious nurse" (e.g. Lady Capulet and the Nurse in *Romeo and Juliet*). He also differentiated among the different professions, "roving merchant" and "prosperous farmer". These categories can be multiplied *ad infinitum*. In other words, the diction must suit the person who is speaking. Accordingly, in later Elizabethan drama, diction became highly specialised. As M.C. Bradbrook has said:

> The specific style for princes, for lovers, for clowns, was fixed.[2]

Whatever kind of style the poet is using, he must always keep certain things in mind. Not only must the diction be realistic in accordance with the speaker, it must also be such as to persuade the reader or audience as well as reach his feelings:

> The Elizabethan dramatist's style is one of impassioned poetic rhetoric, the two commonest functions of which are to persuade and to touch the emotions.[3]

It has also been pointed out by classical theorists that the poet should make use of rhetorical devices. Aristotle, in the very definition of tragedy itself, points out that this is an indispensable part of poetic diction. The style may be the grand, or the middle, or the low style, according to the content and the speaker, but it should make use of embellishments. A study of Ben Jonson's *The Alchemist* clarifies this aspect. The low style has been used in it, as the main characters come from the lowest rungs of the social ladder, but when Sir Epicure Mammon speaks Jonson employs the high style. In both the cases he uses figure of speech.

Not only the classical writers, but, following them the English writers, too, have recommended the use of figures of speech. George Puttenham, the Elizabethan rhetorician, had declared:

> There is nothing so fitte for the poem as to be furnished with all the figures that be Rhetoricall and such as do most beautifie the language with eloquence.[4]

Many other theories have been advanced by the classical and later rhetoricians. Horace, for example, recommends the use of newly-coined words as well as the revival of out-of-mode words. Shakespeare has made use of all the ideas known in his time so that the style becomes rich and effective.

Diction in *The Tempest*

Shakespeare's dramatic career stretches over quite a long period, *i.e.*, over two decades, and it is a period of continuous development for him. His art matured more and more as the years passed, and riper years reached higher peaks of excellence. His style developed as much as did his art of characterization, plot-management and other elements. *The Tempest* is the last and the maturest product of his art and in it he has employed a diction eminently suited to the kind of play it is—a romance. Moreover, he adopts all the conventions of style of Elizabethan drama and shows how the conventions can be used to serve his own artistic purposes. The using of a mixture of prose and verse serves to distinguish the noble from the humble characters, as indeed is to be found in all Elizabethan dramatists. Moreover it was also one of the requirements of poetic style that the diction be suited to the action taking place on the stage. This goes back to Aristotle himself:

> ...Language enriched in a variety of ways and artistic devices appropriate to the several parts of the play.[5]

This implies that the same character must not speak in the same manner in different situations. Gonzalo, for example, speaks in simple prose in the first scene when a storm is raging and all of them are in danger of their lives. The same Gonzalo speaks in measured and sophisticated verse when he is talking about his vision of utopia to Alonso and the others. Caliban, when cursing Prospero uses abusive language and yet speaks one of the most poetic passages when describing the music of the island. Ariel's language, indeed, is specially remarkable for its beauty and lightness. Some of the important stylistic devices employed in *The Tempest* shall be studied and as there are a few prose passages they shall be studied separately.

Stylistic Devices

There are many kinds of stylistic devices, imagery, symbols and figures of speech being the most important ones. Of these, imagery and symbolism have already been studied in the preceding chapter and now a few of the most important figures of speech used by the poet will be taken up. A few of the figures used in Act I, sc. ii will be pointed out, as was done in the case of imagery.

Similes are plentifully used and are the most obvious ones for a student to recognise. Thus Miranda, referring to her memory of her infancy, says:

> 'Tis far off
> And rather like a dream than an assurance
> That my memory warrants.[6]

Towards the end of the scene Prospero, addressing Ariel, says:

> Thou shalt be as free
> As mountain winds, but then exactly do.
> All points of my command.[7]

These two very simple similes make use of ordinary well-known images, yet both are noteworthy because of their appropriateness. Miranda's memory of her childhood is dim, just as the memory of a dream is. Ariel is an airy spirit, so the simile of the wind from the mountains is peculiarly apt.

Metaphors have always been regarded as being extremely important figures of speech. Thus Miranda, in her opening speech, uses a metaphor to describe the tumult of the elements in a storm:

But that the sea climbing to the welkin's cheek
Dashes the fire out.[8]

Here the metaphor is not a very clear one. The sky is being compared with a face. A much clearer metaphor occurs when Prospero speaks of himself as a big tree and of his brother as an ivy:

...now he was
The ivy which had hid my princely trunk,
And suck'd my verdure.[9]

This is actually a double metaphor, for here two metaphors are used, Prospero being a tree which supports the ivy, his brother. One of the finest metaphors in the play occurs in a single line:

What seest thou else
In the dark backward and abysm of time.[10]

This metaphor is so extraordinarily effective as here an abstract concept, that of time, is being juxtaposed with the concreteness of an abyss.

Just as similes and metaphors serve to heighten the appeal of poetry, so rhetorical questions give a dramatic effect. Prospero, in mock anger, chides Miranda:

What,
An advocate for an imposter? Hush![11]

This is addressed to Miranda, but often a rhetorical question is not addressed to anyone. It serves to point out the state of the speaker's mind. Thus Prospero wonders at Miranda's remembering that she used to have many women to tend to her:

Thou hadst, and more, Miranda; but how is't
That this lives in thy memory?[12]

This rhetorical question is different from the first in that the former one heightens the dramatic quality of the verse, but the second one is contemplative. In this part of the scene the mood is a reminiscent one, so the tone of musing is quite in keeping with the mood. The versatile property of this figure of speech has been fully realised and used by the poet.

Like the rhetorical question, personification, apostrophe and pathetic fallacy also appeal to the imagination, and all of these have been used in this scene. There is a fine instance of personification when Prospero answers Miranda's question as to why the storm had been raised:

> bountiful Fortune
> Now my dear lady, hath mine enemies
> Brought to this shore.[13]

There are several other personifications in this long scene, as for example in Miranda's opening speech in which the sky is personified. This figure of speech adds pictorial quality to poetry:

> The sky, it seems, would pour down stinking pitch
> But that the sea, mounting to th' welkin's cheek
> Dashes the fire out.[14]

Apostrophe, another figure of speech that enhances the dramatic quality of poetry, has been used repeatedly. The heavenly powers have been apostrophised again and again, mostly by Miranda:

> O, the heavens!
> What foul play had we that we came from thence?[15]

Apostrophes are usually put in the beginning of sentences. In this scene we have one of the rare examples of an apostrophe in the middle of one:

> ...and bend
> The dukedom yet unbow'd—alas, poor Milan—
> to most ignoble stooping[16]

Pathetic fallacy is a figure of speech that appeals to the imagination and also moves the affections, and there are many in this scene:

> To cry to the sea that roar'd to us, to sigh
> To th' winds, whose poity, sighing back again
> Did us but loving wrong.[17]

There are two pathetic fallacies here. The sea is roaring to Prospero and Miranda and the wind is sighing with pity. The passage, in the phrase "loving wrong", also gives an example of oxymoron in which two mutually contradictory qualities are brought together in the same phrase.

Like the oxymoron, antithesis is also a figure based on contradiction and has been used extensively by Shakespeare. Thus, earlier in the same speech as quoted above, Prospero describes the actions of his brother and Alonso:

> With colour fairer painted their foul ends.[18]

In addition to the antithesis in this line, there is also a metaphor—that of a painting. Earlier in the same speech Prospero says:

> By foul play, as thou say'st were we heaved thence,
> But blessedly holp hither.[19]

In addition to figures of speech there are many other stylistic devices like allusions, use of proverb, etc. Allusions can be of many types. A very popular allusion, easy to understand for contempories but difficult for others, are topical allusions, *i.e.* those that refer to contemporary events. There are many such in the play. In this scene for example, Shakespeare is obviously describing the miseries suffered by the fleet of ships in 1609 (*Vide* Ch. 9, the section on sources, *supra*):

> a brave vessel—
> Which had, no doubt, some noble creatures in her—
> Dash'd all to pieces.[20]

These lines, in particular, refer to the total destruction of the ship *Sea-Adventure*. Later, Ariel describes how he had frightened everyone by transforming himself into flames and dividing himself so that the flames burnt in several places at once:

> ...now on the beak
> Now in the waist, the deck, in every cabin
> I flam'd amazement. Sometimes I'd divide
> And burn in many places.[21]

This refers to what sailors call St. Elmo's fire, described by Strachey in his account of the terrible storm:

> ...a little round light, like a faint star, trembling and streaming along with a sparkling blaze, half the height upon the main mast.[22]

Apart from topical allusions there are classical and Biblical allusions as well. Classical allusions (*i.e.* allusions to classical myths and literary works) have been used by Ariel in the given passage.

> Jove's lightnings, the precursors,
> O'th' dreadful thunder-claps, more momentary
> And sight—outrunning were not, the fire and cracks.
> Of sulphurous roaring the most mighty Neptune
> Seem to besiege and make his bold waves tremble.[23]

As one of the appellations of Jove is "the thunderer" and Neptune is the god of the sea the allusions are particularly apt. Many more classical allusions, like these, occur in the play and the masque is entirely made up of classical goddesses.

Another kind of allusion is the Biblical allusion and these are numerous in the play. In this scene also there are several. Caliban refers to the sun and the moon:

> and teach me how
> To name the bigger light and how the less,
> That burn by day and night.[24]

This reference is to be traced to the *Bible*:

> And God made two great lights; the greater one to rule the day, and the lesser light to rule the night.[25]

Biblical allusions, indeed, permeate the work, sometimes conscious and sometimes unconscious. Prospero, for example, tells Miranda:

> O, a cherubim
> Thou wast that didst preserve me.[26]

Cherubims are spiritual entities, occurring again and again in the *Bible*. It should be remembered that according to mediaeval theory of angelology there are nine orders of angels and cherubims are the second highest of them.

Another stylistic device is the use of proverbs and saws, and Shakespeare makes frequent use of them. Later in the play the two comic characters repeatedly use them. In this scene Prospero, referring to his brother, says, blaming himself:

and my trust
Like a good parent, did beget of him,
A falsehood.[27]

Here Prospero is referring to the proverb. "Great men's sons seldom do well". So does Miranda when, asked to comment on Antonio, she says:

I should sin
To think but nobly of my grandmother:
Good wombs have borne bad sons.[28]

These are only a few of the stylistic devices used by Shakespeare. It should be remembered that close analysis will reveal many more of them.

(b) Versification

As has been pointed out at the very beginning of this chapter, diction and versification are the two sides of the same coin. Any discussion of a poet's style is incomplete without a discussion of versification. A knowledge of prosody is essential for understanding this highly technical aspect of poetry. As Henri Fluchère has pointed out:

> It is by its rhythm as much as by its images that a verse is expressive. The rhythmical succession has an emotional pattern, shows a purpose, imposing a mood or defining a thought.[29]

The metre used in Elizabethan drama was blank verse, though couplets were frequently employed. Blank verse passages consist of lines of unrhyming iambic pentametre lines, that is, five iambic feet. Iambic is a disyllabic metre, of which the first is unstressed and the second is stressed:

L̆ie thére m̆y art/wip̆e thóu/th̆ine eyés hăve cŏm/fŏrt.

The díre/fŭl spéctăcle óf/th̆e wréck/whích toúch'd

T̆he vé/rў vír/tŭe óf/ cŏmpás/sion ĭn thée,

Ĭ háve wĭth/ súch/ prŏvi/siŏn ín / m̆ine árt.[30]

This passage has four lines, not rhyming in any way. The majority of the feet are iambic, though there is an anapaest in line number three. Such irregularities are often to be found in dramatic blank verse. In fact such variations add to the flexibility of a blank verse passage. Absolutely regular blank verse is difficult to find in plays.

There are many complex features of versification. One such feature is the use of end-stopped and of run-on lines. In the passage given above the first line has a full-stop at the end, *i.e.* the actor will have to pause there for a short time. This is an end-stopped line. On the other hand the second line has no punctuation-marks at the end and the actor will have to go on to speak the next line without any pause. Such a line is called a run-on line. These devices help avoid monotony. Run-on lines give smoothness to the passage, whereas a succession of end-stopped lines tend to make verse rather jerky.

This, however, does not mean that end-stopped lines should always be avoided. An artist like him can make use of end-stopped lines in order to enhance the beauty of his versification. This is how Gonzalo describes his utopia:

no name of magistrate;
Letters should not be known; riches, poverty,
And use of service, none; contract, succession,
Bourn, bound of land, tilth, vinyard, none;
No use of metal, corn, or wine, or oil;
No occupation, all men idle, all,
And women too, but innocent and pure.[31]

Here Gonzalo is giving a catalogue of all the features to be found in his utopia. These features have to be emphasised, and this emphasis is achieved by definite pauses at the end of each line. Had the lines been run-on ones, the catalogue would not have been so impressive.

Every line has a short pause within it, which is known as the caesura or the medial pause. The placing of the caesura in the line is an important factor in the excellence of blank verse. It used to be the custom earlier (in mediaeval poetry like *Piers Plowman,* for example) to place the caesura always in the middle of the line. This gave the verse a mechanical and monotonous quality which should be avoided at all costs in dramatic blank verse. The Elizabethan dramatists took the actor's convenience into consideration. They placed the caesura, not in the middle of the line, but anywhere in the line in such a way that the actor would be easily able to recite it. Thus Prospero reminisces about Milan:

> Through all the signories || it was the first,
> And Prospero the prime duke || being so reputed
> In dignity, || and for liberal arts
> Without a parallel; || those being all my study.[32]

The double vertical lines indicate the caesura. This is how it falls:

> Line 1—after the sixth syllable
> Line 2—after the seventh syllable
> Line 3—after the fourth syllable
> Line 4—after the sixth syllable

This variation renders the lines flexible. Sometimes there are two caesurae. Thus in the lines preceding the ones quoted above, we have:

> My brother, || and thy uncle, || call'd Antonio.[33]

Double caesurae are not so common, but they are sometimes used to emphasize some words.

Blank verse, by definition, contains ten syllables in each line, but this is not an inflexible rule. A line may very often have more than ten syllables in it:

> An̆d t́o/my̆ státe/grĕw strań/gĕr, beińg/tran̆spórted.[34]

The line has an extra syllable, so there is a total of eleven syllables in the line. Likewise one may have less than ten syllables in a line. The most important of such short lines in this play is Prospero answer to Miranda's question:

> By̆ ṕro/vĭdeńce/dĭvińe;—[35]

This wonderful line has only three feet in it, and there is a long pause at the end, emphasizing the inexplicable quality of God's mercy.

This short and sketchy account makes it clear that really good dramatic blank verse can never be regular iambic pentametre. There are many other devices to give flexibility to the lines which are too technical to be discussed here. One such will, however, have to be mentioned.

Very often, particularly in conversation, a line is broken up to escape monotony. This technique is known as stichomythia and is often used by Shakespeare to introduce variety:

Prospero : I prize above my dukedom.
Miranda : Would I might
But ever see that man!
Prospero : Now I arise.[36]

Two consecutive lines have been broken up here between two speakers. As this dialogue is very long, there are frequent examples of this technique, which saves the verse from being monotonous.

No discussion of versification can be complete without a study of the songs. Music is an essential part of drama, one of its six elements as given by Aristotle. Elizabethan dramatists used both vocal and instrumental music in their plays and this play is permeated with both of these. John P. Cutts, after studying the music of this play, remarks:

> No other play...portrays such an extensive and uniform treatment of music.[37]

There are, in all, nine songs in the play, five of them sung by Ariel. There are, in addition, numerous pieces of mood-music scattered throughout the play. Instrumental music plays a very important part in the play. As a matter of fact, both of these kinds of music form the very nature of the island, permeating its atmosphere. Caliban, in one of the best passages in the play, says:

> ...the isld is full of noises,
> Sounds, and sweet airs, that give delight, and hurt not
> Sometimes a thousand twangling instruments
> Will hum about mine ears; and sometime voices.[38]

Throughout the play, again and again, there are stage-directions about music and this music serves many purposes. A solemn music, played by Ariel, puts the royal party to sleep in the first scene of the second Act. In the feast-scene there is "solemn and strange music" when the banquet is spread and after Ariel vanishes there is soft music again. The masque has instrumental as well as vocal music, providing the duet sung by Juno and Ceres.

Two of Ariel's songs are sung in the second scene of the play: "Come unto these yellow sands" and "Full fathom five". The first of these soothes Ferdinand and calms the storm. It is a song that emphasizes harmony, peace and love. The singer invites the listener to join hands and dance, along with spirits. What is more, dogs and a cock provide the refrain. In other words, loving and merry relationship is established among man, animal and spirits. All are brought together under the peaceful aegis of music.

The next song "Full fathom five" is unique in its apparent simplicity and hidden depth of meaning:

> Full fathom five thy father lies;
> Of his bones are coral made;
> Those are pearls that were his eyes;
> Nothing of him that doth fade,
> But doth suffer a sea-change
> Into something rich and strange.[39]

The lines have a childlike simplicity which is totally deceptive and specially apt for Ariel, who is a childlike spirit himself. This is true of all his songs, but the depth of meaning in this song is unique. The sea is seen as a benevolent entity that transforms mortal remains into objects of precious and immortal beauty. As a lyric it does not have its equal in depth of meaning and beauty of imagery. It is only the mature art of Shakespeare that can produce a lyric like this. Life and death, nature, man and the supernatural (sea-nymphs) are all brought together in harmonious beauty.

Ariel's next song is highly functional for it awakens the sleeping Gonzalo to foil the murder-plot. His next song is sung to Prospero, in high spirits, to show how quick he can be. His fifth and the last song of the play is sung in the last scene. It is a song of pure joy, anticipating his freedom from servitude. It comprises a quintette followed by a couplet. The quintette is remarkable in that it uses only one rhyme in its five lines.

Besides the songs of Ariel there are four other songs. The fourth song of the play is sung by Trinculo—a licentious song sung by a drunkard. The next song in this scene is sung by Caliban when he too is drunk and it has been pointed out that it is like a nursery rhyme. These two songs, very different from the ones sung by Ariel, serve the comic purpose very effectively and so does the next song sung by these comic characters in Act III, scene ii. They sing it out of tune and Caliban is aware of this fact. Ariel then plays the tune while himself remaining invisible.

The masque, coming in the fourth Act, is in a class by itself. As has been pointed out (in Ch. 9, Plot, *supra*) it fulfils one of the requirements as demanded by Aristotle—that of "opsis" or spectacle.

It is a colourful musical entertainment, but it is not merely an entertainment. It serves an important dramatic purpose, for it solemnises and celebrates the betrothal of Ferdinand and Miranda. The spirits of the island play the roles of three goddesses: Iris, Ceres and Juno. These three, respectively, symbolise harmony, plenty and marriage-bliss, and bless the happy couple.

The speeches of the goddesses are in heroic couplets. Elizabethan plays make frequent use of this measure and so does Shakespeare, specially at the ends of scenes, in order to highlight a moral message or the theme. Such couplets, known as "Senecan sententiae", have been used but once in this play. The masque, however, is entirely in heroic couplets except for the song of blessing. This is a song sung by Juno and Ceres and is in couplets of trochaic tetrametres:

> Hónoŭr/riches/márriâge/bléssiňg
>
> Lóng cŏn/tińuănce/ańd iň/créasing
>
> Hourly joys be still upon you!
> Juno sings her blessings on you[40]

Music, both instrumental and vocal, thus plays a very important role and fulfils several functions in this play. It creates the proper atmosphere and the right mood. It calms the wildness of the sea and the wildness of grief in Ferdinand's heart and prevents murder.

The different aspects of poetic style, as seen above, form one of the facets of the play. In this chapter all the examples of figures of speech and metre have been taken from one scene only—the second scene of Act I, as had been done with images also. The earnest student will realise what variety and wealth of imagery and rhetoric can be found in the rest of the play if a systematic study is undertaken. This is a very sketchy study.

REFERENCES

1. Dorsch, T.S., ed. and transl., *Classical Literary Criticism,* Penguin Books, 1975, p. 83.
2. Bradbrook, M.C., *op. cit.,* p. 45.
3. Fluchère, H., *op. cit.,* p. 152.
4. Quoted by Fluchère, *op. cit.,* p. 159.
5. Dorsch, T.S., *op. cit.,* p. 39.
6. Act I, sc. ii, *ll.* 44-46, p. 6.
7. Act I, sc. ii, *ll.* 499-501, p. 25.
8. Act I, sc. ii, *ll.* 4-5, p. 4.
9. Act I, sc. ii, *ll.* 86-87, pp. 7-8.
10. Act I, sc. ii, *ll.* 49-50, p. 6.
11. Act I, sc. ii, *ll.* 477-78, p. 24.
12. Act I, sc. ii, *ll.* 48-49, p. 6.
13. Act I, sc. ii, *ll.* 178-90, pp. 11-12.
14. Act I, sc. ii, *ll.* 3-5, p. 4.
15. Act I, sc. ii, *ll.* 59-60, p. 6.
16. Act I, sc. ii, *ll.* 114-16, p. 9.
17. Act I, sc. ii, *ll.* 149-51, p. 10.
18. Act I, sc. ii, *ll.* 143, p. 10.
19. Act I, sc. ii, *ll.* 62-63, p. 6.
20. Act I, sc. ii, *ll.* 6-8, p. 4.
21. Act I, sc. ii, *ll.* 196-98, p. 12.
22. Chapter 9, section on the sources, *supra.*

23. Act I, sc. ii, *ll.* 201-05, p. 12.
24. Act I, sc. ii, *ll.* 334-36, p. 18.
25. *Genesis*, Chapter 1, verse 16. *The Holy Bible*, N.Y., American Book Society, no date. p. 1.
26. Act I, sc. ii, *ll.* 152-53, p. 11.
27. Act I, sc. ii, *ll.* 93-95, p. 8.
28. Act I, sc. ii, *ll.* 118-20, p. 9.
29. Fluchère, H., *op. cit.*, p. 181.
30. Act I, sc. ii, *ll.* 25-28, p. 5.
31. Act II, sc. i, *ll.* 146-52, p. 33.
32. Act I, sc. ii, *ll.* 71-74, p. 7.
33. Act I, sc. ii, *l.* 66, p. 7.
34. Act I, sc. ii, *l.* 76, p. 7.
35. Act I, sc. ii, *l.* 159, p. 11.
36. Act I, sc. ii, *ll.* 168-69, p. 11.
37. Cutts, John, P., *Music and the Supernatural in The Tempest*, in Palmer, *op. cit.*, p. 209.
38. Act III, sc. ii, *ll.* 133-36, p. 57.
39. Act I, sc. ii, *ll.* 397-92, p. 21.
40. Act IV, sc. i, *ll.* 106-9, p. 69.

12

Critical Reception: A Brief History

The Tempest, the last play to be written entirely by Shakespeare, was a highly popular play in its own time as well as later. The first record of its performance tells us that it was produced at Court on the first of November, 1611:

> Hallomas nyght was presented att Whithall before ye kings Majestie, a play called the Tempest.[1]

It was performed again at Court next year as part of the celebrations entertaining and blessing a royal marriage and Shakespeare himself is said to have enacted the role of Prospero.

It is a play that has been a universal favourite, with stage-managers as well as literary critics. Dryden had pointed out the inimitable beauty of the play:

> But Shakespeare's Magick could not copy'd be;
> Within that circle none durst walk but he.[2]

The characteristic taste of the Restoration audience demanded a different treatment, so Dryden and Davenant re-formed the play, giving Miranda a sister and providing her with a partner. Ariel and Caliban, too, have, not been deprived. They have their female counterparts.

In the seventeenth and the eighteenth centuries the philosophical aspect of the play was ignored. These critics kept Ben Jonson's declaration in mind, that Shakespeare did not have have much classical learning. So they laid stress upon the inventive power of his imagination. Addison pointed out:

> It shows a greater genius in Shakespeare to have drawn his Caliban than his Hotspur or Julius Caesar: the one

> was to be supplied out of his own imagination, whereas the other might have been formed upon tradition, history and observation.[3]

With the coming of the Romantics the focus shifted. They looked upon the play as an expression of deep and subtle ideas, too subtle for the stage. They laid more emphasis on its poetic beauty than on its stage-worthiness. This attitude continued into the Victorian age. These critics became conscious of the importance of chronology and gave autobiographical interpretation of the play. Thus Dowden looks upon the play as reflecting the calm vision of maturity. It also has to be remembered that Dowden recognised a unified them in it. He was the first to do so:

> A thought which seems to run through the whole of *The Tempest*, appearing here and there like a coloured thread in some web, is the thought that the true freedom of man consists in service.[4]

Dowden projects an image of Shakespeare as a benevolent old man like Prospero, blessing the happiness of a younger generation, but himself remaining at a distance from all emotional turmoils. Strachey takes another view, that in *The Tempest* Shakespeare is bored with everything—both in life and in literature. This is not the general attitude of the twentieth century critics.

In the twentieth century the critics took the play extremely seriously, painstakingly analysing all the different aspects. The theme of the play has provoked serious thought among them and the plot has been taken up as embodying his assurance of the validity of repentance and forgiveness, of rebirth and renewal of life (*Vide* Ch. 6, *supra*). The last romances are seen to be integrally related to the seasonal cycle of Nature—the cycle of birth, growth, death and rebirth. So Prospero breaks his staff and buries his book deeper than ever did plummet sound, and a purer life is carried on by Ferdinand and Miranda. E.M.W. Tillyard relates this play to the tragic pattern and finds the completion of a cycle in which tragic disorder reaches final harmony.

Revival of interest in the Elizabethan beliefs and stage conventions have led to different kinds of analyses of Shakespearean plays and *The Tempest* has provided much food for thought. Theodore Spencer shows how Shakespeare reflects the prevailing Elizabethan attitude to man and the cosmos. He takes into account the psychological, philosophical and religious beliefs of the Elizabethans and comes to the conclusion:

> In this last of his complete plays...Shakespeare uses, however unconsciously, the common body of psychological assumptions that was given him by his time.[5]

Thus Spencer shows how in this play Shakespeare takes into account the conventional view of the levels of hierarchy in Nature—the animal, the human and the intellectual and shows the relationship between them.

Likewise, Elizabethan stage conventions are taken into account and the play is interpreted according to Shakespeare's adaptation of them. The masque of *The Tempest* is given as an example of his masterly skill in adopting a fashionable custom and adapting it to serve his own purposes—blending the concept of a new and purer life with colourful entertainment.

Different aspects of the play have come under the spotlight. Characters and Plot had already been under discussion from the very beginning and now other aspects like imagery, symbolism, etc. are also being studied. Thus Caroline Spurgeon and W. Clemen have made extensive studies of the images used, tracing the development of his imagery from the earliest to the last plays. Thus Clemen finds that in this play the imagery used is not only decorative but is highly functional, fulfilling many dramatic purposes. Moreover, certain images have been taken up and studied as the ruling motifs of Shakespeare's plays—tempest standing for destruction and music for harmony. G. Wilson Knight has made valuable contribution in the field of Shakespeare criticism by taking up these two symbols and studying their recurrence in the plays.

Different characters have been taken up and given new interpretations. Thus, by different critics, Prospero's character has been shown as Shakespeare himself, as representing Art, as typifying the Elizabethan concept of the rational soul, as "man moving towards the realization of the greatest Renaissance ideal". Likewise, each of the other characters also has been differently interpreted. Caliban, for example, is seen as animality, earthiness, the passions, the vegetable soul, the dispossessed inhabitant of an invaded country, etc. (*Vide* Ch. 7, *supra.*)

Not only the characters, but the plot also has been revealed in many different ways by the modern, *i.e.* the twentieth-century critics. The old classical rules have been reviewed and the plot judged from this point of view. Apart from this, different critics have viewed the plot differently. E.M.W. Tillyard, for example, finds the play to be a concentrated trilogy and R.A. Brower finds that there are six "continuities" that recur throughout the play and determine its structure. (These have been mentioned in Ch. 9, Plot, *supra.*)

Many new critical theories have come into existence in the second half of the twentieth century: structuralism, post-structuralism, reception theory, post-colonialism and many more. Many of Shakespeare's works have been interpreted in the light of these theories. The interpretation that looks upon Prospero as the usurper of Caliban's kingdom (*i.e.*, the island which he inherited from his mother) is a post-colonial one. There is textual basis for such a view (*Vide* Ch. 9, *supra*). A recent development in Indian criticism is to interpret the play in the light of classical Indian theories. A brief analysis of this kind is given below.

Indian Interpretation

There are many classical Indian theories of poetry and drama which can be easily applied to Shakespeare as well as other writers. The theories of *alaṅkrā, dhvani, rasa, vakroti,* all reveal different aspects of Shakespeare's poetry. A very brief and sketchy analysis of *The Tempest* will now be given. The rules expounded by Ācārya Dhananjaya in his *Daśarūpakam* are the ones which shall be followed.

According to Indian dramaturgy there are ten kinds of

plays. The second of these is *nātikā* and our play can be put within this category. Usually in such cases the story is a well-known one and so are the characters, but this rule is not an inflexible one and the story need not be well-known or *Prakhyāta*. In the case of *The Tempest* both the story and the characters are the products of the poet's own imagination (*utpādya*). The main or *angī-rasa* of *nātikās* is usually love or *śṛṅgāra*. We face some difficulty in determining the chief or *angī-rasa* of our play. It is true that romantic love does exist in *The Tempest* and is given importance also; we would still hesitate to call it the *angī* or the central theme of the play. It will have been seen in Chapter 6 that many themes have been suggested for the play but love is not the most important of them as it is in his golden comedies. It is repentance-forgiving-and-reconciliation that has been emphasised as the most important theme and leaves a lasting impression on the mind of the reader. It is not possible or proper to say that love or *śṛṅgāra* is the *angī-rasa* of the play. This is the only respect in which *The Tempest* falls short of being a true *nātikā*.

The plots of drama can be divided into two main sections: the *adhikārika* and the *prāsaṅgika*. The first of these is the main plot and the second the sub-plot. This latter is again divided into two kinds: the *pātākā* and the *prakarī*. In our play the difference between the plots is quite a well-marked one. The main story is concerned with Prospero, Miranda and the other courtly characters while Stephano, Trinculo and Caliban make up the *prāsangika*. This sub-plot can be called a *pātākā*, for it continues till the very end of the play, but the murder-plots of Antonio and of Caliban are *prakarīs* for both of them exist only for a very short time. Other such episodes like the banquet-scene, the log-bearing scene, the masque, will all be called *prakarī* also.

The heroes of Sanskrit plays have been divided mainly into four categories, the third of which is the *dhīrodātta nāyaka*. Ācārya Dhananjaya defines such a hero thus:

> Mahāsattvo-atigambhīrah kṣamāvānāvikatthana
> Sthiro nigurha-ahaṅkāro dhīrodātta dṛrhavrata

> The self-controlled and exalted hero is of great excellence, exceedingly serious, forbearing, not boastful, resolute, with self-assurance and firm of purpose.[6]

Prospero's character fulfils all these requirements though it must be said here that according to Ācārya Dhananjaya the hero of a *nātikā* should be a dhīra-lalita hero. Such a hero can be found in him who, after all, is the romantic hero of the play:

> Niścinto dhīralalitah kalāsaktah sukhīmṛdu—The self-controlled and light-hearted hero is free from anxiety, fond of the arts, happy and gentle.[7]

Ferdinand, when we see him first, is downcast with sorrow for the supposed death of his father, but he recovers from it very quickly; that is, he is not by nature a worried and anxious man. So the epithet *niścinta* suits his nature. As to whether he is *kalāsaktah* or not we are not able to judge, for he does not ask specially for music as Orsino the ideal *dhīralalitah* hero does. He, however, has a soul that responds to Ariel's music and is also genuinely pleased by the masque. His nature is of a happy (sukhī) and gentle (mṛduh) disposition as his behaviour to Miranda exemplifies.

The heroines have been classified into numerous sections and one such basic division is the one of *svīyā* and *parakīyā*. According to this our heroine will be *svīyā* heroine for she is not another man's wife like a *parakīyā* heroine. According to the development of the sentiment of love in her heart, she can, at first, be called a *mugdhā* heroine who quickly develops into a *madhyā* one when she declares her love. In the last scene, when she laughingly accuses Ferdinand of cheating her at chess, she is definitely a madhyā heroine. At first she is overwhelmed by her love but, deterred by Prospero's presence, cannot declare it. Later in the log-bearing scene she declares her love quite openly. This development of love in her leads us to the graces (*alankāras*) that heroines should have. There are twenty-seven of these graces and the first three of them deal with the state of the heroine's mind. *Bhāva* is the first appearance of love in her mind, and we find this when she sees Ferdinand for the first time. The other, more developed stages of love, like *hāva* and *hela* are also to be found in her. The other graces, like *śobhā, kānti, dīpti,* etc. deal with the physical and mental beauties of the heroine and many of them are to be found in her, if a detailed study is made.

Sanskrit poetics offers great scope for analysing and interpreting Shakespeare's plays, and the serious student will find that such studies add to our understanding and enjoyment of his poetry, which are the two important functions of criticism according to T.S. Eliot.

REFERENCES

1. Quoted in Palmer, *op. cit.*, p. 11.
2. Kinsley, J., ed., *The Poems and Fables of John Dryden*, London, Oxford Univ. Press, 1970, p. 117.
3. Palmer, *op. cit.*, p. 18.
4. Dowden, *op. cit.*, p. 75.
5. Spencer, T., *op. cit.*, p. 195.
6. Haas, C.O., transl., *The Daśarūpa*, N.Y., Columbia Univ. Press, 1912, p. 41.
7. *Ibid.*

Important Questions

1. What part does the theme of freedom in servitude play in *The Tempest*? Discuss.
2. Do you agree that the play shows Prospero's limitations as well as his virtues? Give reasons in support of your answers.
3. How does Shakespeare arouse sympathetic feelings towards Caliban? Discuss.
4. Examine the relationship between the main plot and the sub-plot in *The Tempest.*
5. Analyse the function of the Masque in the play.
6. Do you agree with the view that Prospero controls the action of the play? Give reasons for your answer.
7. Write a note on the function of music in the play.
8. "The poet rises still higher in his management of the character of Ariel, by making a moral use of it." Elucidate.
9. "He has carried the romantic, the wonderful and the wild, to the most pleasing extravagances." Justify.
10. "The action is one, great and entire: the restoration of Prospero to his dukedom." Examine the play in the light of this remark.
11. "Caliban is in some respects a noble being; the poet has raised him far above contempt." Elucidate.
12. Coleridge calls the second sc. of Act I the "finest piece of retrospective narration." Do you agree?

13. Comment critically on the remark: "The appearance of super or ultra-natural servants are finely contrasted."
14. "The language was not drawn from any set fashion but from the profoundest depths of his moral being." Examine the poetic style of the play in the light of this remark.
15. "The human and the imaginary characters, the dramatic and the grotesque, are blended together with the greatest art." Justify.
16. Write a note on *The Tempest* as a romance.
17. Can *The Tempest* be called a pastoral comedy? Give reasons for your answer.
18. Analyse Miranda's character as a heroine of the Last Romances.
19. Discuss the theme of "reconciliation, with pardon and atonement for the sins of one generation in the young love of children."
20. Analyse the function of imagery in the play.

A Select Bibliography

Bradbrook, M.C., *The Growth and Structure of Elizabethan Comedy,* London: Chatto & Windus, 1955.

——, *Elizabethan Stage Conditions*. Cambridge: The University Press, 1968.

Brown, J.R., *Shakespeare and His Comedies,* London: Methuen, 1957.

Bullough, G., *Narrative and Dramatic Sources of Shakespeare,* London: Routledge and Kegan Paul, 1958.

Champion, L.S., *The Evolution of Shakespeare's Comedies,* Harvard: The University Press, 1973.

Charlton, H.B., *Shakespeare's Comedies,* London: Methuen, 1977.

Clemen, W., *The Development of Shakespeare's Imagery,* London: Methuen, 1977.

Fluchère, H., *Shakespeare*, London: Longman's Green & Com., 1953.

Knight, G.W., *The Shakespearean Tempest*, London: Meth., 1953.

Palmer, D.J., ed., *The Tempest: A Casebook,* London: Macmillan, 1968.

Ribner, I., *William Shakespeare: Life, Times and Theatre,* New Delhi: Wiley Eastern Ltd., 1978.

Sengupta, S.C., *Shakespearean Comedy*. London: OUP, 1950.

Tillyard, E.M.W., *The Elizabethan World Picture*, New York: Vintage Books, no date.

Index